To Melisa

Thank for all
your great help

Paul

HOPE
AND A FUTURE

Life, Survival, and Renewal
on the Streets of an African Slum

PAUL HIGDON

LITTLE
BOOST
PRESS

Scripture taken from the Holy Bible, NEW INTERNATIONAL VERSION®. Copyright © 1973, 1978, 1984, 2011 by Biblica, Inc. All rights reserved worldwide. Used by permission. NEW INTERNATIONAL VERSION® and NIV® are registered trademarks of Biblica, Inc. Use of either trademark for the offering of goods or services requires the prior written consent of Biblica US, Inc.

Scripture taken from the King James Version of the Bible.

ISBN: 978-1-7346288-0-7 (sc)
ISBN: 978-1-7346288-1-4 (e)

Little Boost Press rev. date: 3/19/2020

TO LINDA

my wife; my companion in adventure;
and, above all, the greatest spirit,
whose heart is open to all of life

All royalties from the sale of this book
are dedicated to the benefit of disadvantaged children
in the United States and overseas.

Please visit us at **www.littleboostpress.org**
to see how we are giving children in need a little boost.

Poverty isn't natural; it's manmade.
—Nelson Mandela,
as seen painted on the back of a Kenyan bus

Doing nothing is a great way to change nothing.
—Kid President

CONTENTS

PROLOGUE:
IN A HOSPITAL NEAR NAIROBI

FEBRUARY 2010

John was just beginning to recover from the brutal attack. His head was fully bandaged with only a slit for his eyes. His right arm hung from a sling, wrapped to his elbow. The ICU doctors said he had been in a coma for three days after a driver had brought him in. John was slowly gathering his wits and was told he was going to live, but recuperation in the hospital would take several months.

Haunting images of machetes gleaming through blinding torchlight flashed through his mind, tensing every muscle in his body for a terrifying instant. Wavering in and out of consciousness, he gradually realized he could relax in the safety of his bed.

Relieved that the terrible event was over, he began to wonder where life would take him from here. One thing was certain; he was going to lose his internship at the food processing plant in Nairobi's industrial district because of the time he'd spend in recovery. That job was his one sure avenue out of poverty, out of grinding life on the streets. Now it was gone.

Forlorn, he silently prayed the verse from Jeremiah (29:11 NIV) that he had prayed every day for the past ten years. A secondary school teacher had taught him to recite it every morning as a source of inspiration: "For I know the plans I have for you," declares the Lord, "plans to prosper … and not to harm you, plans to give you hope and a future." As he prayed, he thought to himself, *God, you have been so good to me. You have allowed me to live. So many of my friends have died or given up. I am injured, but I am alive. And now I know you have good plans for me. But please, dear Lord, I beg of you, don't make me live on the streets again, not on the streets again.*

PART I
LOST AND FOUND
——— 2001 and 2013 ———

Talent is universal, opportunity is not.

—Nicholas Kristof

Chapter 1
ONE MORNING IN MATHARE

AUGUST 2001

No one was safe there—not the inhabitants and certainly not a group of middle-aged white folk traipsing through the Nairobi slum. Robberies in broad daylight were common, and foreigners were easy marks—prime targets who the locals thought were loaded with cash. To ensure our safety, young men were assigned to escort us to our destination.

My wife, Linda, and I were members of a group of a dozen Americans on a humanitarian tour sponsored by our church in Chicago. Over the course of three weeks, we would visit philanthropic projects in Kenya and Tanzania—orphanages, water wells, community centers, and trade schools. It was our first day of the trip. We were struggling from jet lag, and our first visit was to an orphanage in the slums.

Two eight-seater vans transported us across Nairobi's modern Central Business District to an abandoned Esso gas station on the edge of a vast shantytown. As we alighted, we saw a troop of young men making its way up the hill. Each fellow peeled off and matched up with one of our group. My companion was a short, wiry young lad with bright eyes and a broad, gap-toothed smile. He grabbed my arm like he'd never let me go. "I'll show you the way, sir," he said.

I sputtered a tense, "Thank you," grateful for his help but too apprehensive about my surroundings to bother to ask his name.

We descended into Mathare, one of the gloriously named "estates" that makes up greater Nairobi. That morning, I had located Mathare on a map in our hotel lobby. It was colored a gentle spring green with a wavy blue line running through it, just how you'd expect a cartographer to depict an elegant estate.

Each member with an escort, our group ambled down a long, sloping track packed on both sides with tiny shops and makeshift wooden platforms. Kiosks carried an incongruous array of items—candies, prepaid cell phone cards, tire irons, and plastic buckets gleaming with colors not found in nature. Fruit stands were stacked with bright yellow bananas, dark-green papayas, and prickly pineapples trucked in from outlying farms. A butcher carefully removed the entrails of a freshly killed goat hung by its hindquarters. The streets in Mathare were too narrow to accommodate cars but wide enough to carry busy crowds and buzzing motorbikes. Rivulets of filth striped our path. Stench buffeted about.

"Be careful, sir," my guide warned. "Look out for the plastic bags." I recalled the mention of "flying toilets" from the pretrip orientation meeting in Chicago. Not only were there no paved sidewalks or streets in Mathare, there was also no electricity and few sewer lines. With limited public sanitation, the locals relieved themselves in plastic bags, tied them tightly, and flung them incautiously into space.

It hadn't rained for weeks, so the track was treacherous with loose gravel. Dust billowed with the footsteps of each passerby. I was walking into one of the most forsaken human habitations on earth. The van was now far behind. As we descended the slope, fear welled within me step by step. Would one of the seemingly friendly inhabitants suddenly turn hostile? Were we just a naive band of white people innocently marching into an African slum? I watched every face apprehensively but made sure never to make eye contact. I calmed myself by recalling an article I had recently read—one of every eight of our fellow mortals lives in urban slums. That rational thought offered a tiny drop of emotional unguent, a momentary salve for my anxiety.

We turned a corner, and the Mathare Estate assaulted my field of vision. Ramshackle cubes of cardboard and tin pressed cheek to jowl as far as the eye could see. The map's spring green was a vast jumble of countless shacks. Drab brown and gray blocks capped with dull gray corrugated metal sheets created a landscape mural without color. No one knew how many people lived in Mathare. I recalled reading somewhere that it was about three hundred thousand. One of the older boys made the fantastical claim that it was one million. Whatever the number, for the one hundred years since the first squatters arrived, Mathare had always been an uneasy cauldron of tribes, migrants from all corners of Kenya reaching for splendid tomorrows but just trying to survive today. It now dawned on me that "estate" was the bureaucratic euphemism assigned to Nairobi's teeming slums. I looked down into the valley and realized that the map's wavy blue line was instead a black stream. Two boys bathed in the septic river.

"Street boys," my guide proudly stated. "They don't have a home like me."

A few steps later, we stood before a massive blue metal gate. We had arrived at the Good Samaritan orphanage. Children's shouts in Swahili— "*Wazungu, wazungu!*" (White people, white people)— announced our arrival. The enormous gate creaked open just long enough for our group to scurry inside; then it quickly banged shut.

Inside the compound, I felt safe at last, a sense of relief to be protected behind iron and brick. Tension drained. I realized that I had been so preoccupied with my own concerns that I had forgotten to ask my guide his name.

"I'm John. John Maina." He smiled proudly.

Once inside, I realized how tall were the walls of the compound. In the next instant, I sensed how small were the grounds, how cramped it all seemed amid boundless Mathare. But the joyous shrieks of the children brought me up and out of myself, bright playfulness melting my dreary obsessions.

Oh, the children's faces beamed to see visitors from afar! They rushed to me. Boys flexed their skinny arms, proudly displaying their small muscles under faded T-shirts—cast-off secondhand garments that had somehow found their way across the ocean. Little girls wearing thin cotton dresses that had seen too many owners swayed side to side, displaying their cute innocence.

It seemed so incongruous. *How can the Mathare slum hold such joy?* I asked myself.

And how we played! The children didn't see many white people and certainly not many with gray hair and a gray beard. I bent down, inviting each of them to open a palm upward. One by one, I took those tiny hands and quickly rubbed them against my beard. "That tickles! More! More! More, mister, more!" Waves of giggles bounced off the metal door.

The children bunched around me, hands reaching out. I thought I'd topple backward, but a gaggle of little ones propped me up from behind. The children touched my straight hair, which they had rarely seen and certainly had never felt. When all had taken their turns and the novelty had worn off, the children scattered, allowing me to rise to my feet. John explained that they were particularly excited because few visitors ever engaged them so closely.

With several more steps into the compound, I could see their sanctuary—no paradise, but at least a safe harbor. The plot of land claimed by the orphanage was a little larger than a basketball court. One half was given over to a two-story wood-and-tin structure, and the other half was an open-air playground. It looked much like the track we had just descended—dusty, light brown soil punctuated by an occasional scraggily weed. Ribbons of wastewater flowed beneath the walls running through the play area. Three hens clucked about, frantically pecking for the odd morsel. The yard had no equipment—no basketball hoop, no soccer net, no bars, no swings or slides. Some older boys enthusiastically kicked a half-deflated soccer ball with a dull thud and limp propulsion. Along the side of the playground were six open stalls, each with a grimy cement floor perforated by a single hole. Fetid brooms stood at attention in each stall.

A short, broad woman draped in a blue-flowered muumuu approached with a deliberate pace. A faded apron wrapped her ample girth. She was wiping her hands from kitchen duties. She offered me her wrist and introduced herself simply as Mama Mercy. I wasn't quite sure who she was, but it was clear that she was an authority inside these walls. I politely thanked her for allowing us to visit and play with the children.

"How many children are there?" I asked.

"By God's grace, one hundred fifteen. If we had more room, I could take three toddlers off the streets every day. But God has already blessed us with great bounty." There was a slight pause before she added, "I see you have John Maina caring for you today. He is a wonderful boy." Turning to him, her eyes softened. "John, please take good care of our guest." She bade me farewell and returned to the kitchen.

Our brief encounter, however pleasant, seemed all too abrupt until I later learned more about Mama Mercy. John told me that she was the matron and founder of the Good Samaritan orphanage, a woman of immense inner strength motivated by a deep faith in God. Her priorities were clear; she was there to care for abandoned children. Although she always graciously received visitors, she was not going to fawn over privileged foreigners with round-trip tickets out of Mathare.

I spent the morning with John. He eventually diverted us from the rest of the group to give me his own personal tour. He tugged my arm, guiding me to the boys' dormitory. Mattresses were packed side to side, front to back. A damp, lived-in odor wafted about. He was sure to point out the bed he slept in. A half dozen battered metal trunks were stacked against the far wall. John proudly showed me his own large rectangular box, measuring fully three cubic feet, which held all his worldly possessions. Little boys, he explained, had nothing more than the clothes on their backs and one plastic bag that an older boy kept for them in his metal trunk. We jogged up creaky wooden stairs to the schoolrooms. John was beaming with excitement to show me the classroom in which study review sessions and special activities were held. I squinted to make out an elaborate diagram on the pockmarked chalkboard, illuminated only by dappled light creeping through uneven clapboard walls. It was the process of photosynthesis.

"We were just reviewing this the other day," John said. "I'd be happy to explain it to you."

I recalled my struggles with photosynthesis in biology class at a suburban high school near Chicago, and here was someone from an African slum offering an explanation. In this budding friendship, I began to see John for who he was—a polite, articulate, well-educated young man in his late teens preparing for college entrance exams, not a scruffy, ill-mannered, uneducated rascal from a Dickens novel that might fit the stereotype of an African slum dweller. *How could this be in Mathare?* As much as my faded scientific knowledge could have used the refresher, I invited him to show me more of his home.

As we walked the few corridors of the orphanage, John told me more about his life. He had a special distinction at Good

Samaritan—he and his half brother were the first children Mama Mercy had taken in. "It was ten years ago," he said, "I was only seven years old. Mama Mercy picked us off the street. That was the beginning of Good Samaritan. I slept in a chicken coop for the first two years until Mama could afford a mattress."

For the past ten years, John had been raised behind the secure walls that held this blessed community of abandoned children. I learned a few details about John's life that morning. But the facts weren't all that important; it was John's gentle behavior and bright energy that captivated me. When we finally rejoined the others in the tour group, I saw John pick up a distressed toddler who had just fallen to his knees. You can tell a lot about a man's spirit when he's holding a baby. John's touch was tender and compassionate.

In such a short time, I took a liking to this young man; he had found a way into my heart. The day had unfolded like a movie. Those few hours I spent with John were cinematic in scope. He had walked me through the vibrancy of Mathare, every sight accented by the cacophony of hawkers, motorbikes, braying animals, and blaring boom boxes. Just as a film director emotionally engages the audience scene by scene with thespian subtleties and evocative musical scores, John led me deeper and deeper into his life in the orphanage. But unlike a movie, which only figuratively takes you by the hand, John had literally taken mine. But where was the script taking me?

At last, our visit was coming to an end. It was time to make our way back to the van. John accompanied me up the hill. I deliberately slowed our pace so we could spend as much time together as possible. We exchanged idle chatter, each word passing the unspoken warmth of friendship.

We arrived at the vehicle. I didn't want to go. I didn't want to leave him behind. We were just getting to know each other. Now it was ending just as our friendship was beginning. I tried to make conversation, stammering lamely, "So, John, what will you do next? What would you like to be?"

Without hesitation, John firmly responded, "I want to be a lawyer."

It pained me to hear those words. John had no parents and no money. He was living in an orphanage in an impoverished country in one of the most appalling slums on earth. It was wrenching to see such talent with so little hope for opportunity. I remembered fumbling and stumbling with life when I was seventeen years old. I remembered counseling our sons at John's age, helping them, as best I could, find their passions. I so wanted to sit with John, to hear his story, to offer advice and encouragement, but the van was loading. I felt helpless. *Oh, God, give me back this morning!*

I looked at John. Before I could speak, he implored, "Please, don't ever forget me."

Words failed. Life's most profound experiences are beyond words.

In the silence, I felt my heart break.

In my entire life, nothing has ever had the impact of John's simple plea. Those several words unleashed feelings deep inside me that I didn't realize were even there.

How many times have I tried to make sense of that haunting instant? Here was a spirited young man whose dreams were colliding with a cruelly indifferent world. As compassion for him swelled in my heart, fright welled from deep within—in life's inscrutable lottery, how was this happening to John? What calamities had landed him in such neglect? I quaked at the very thought of our own two sons, Lars and Nils, fending for themselves on the streets at seven years old. In an abandoned gas station, John and I stood next to each other, the fragility of hope alongside fortuitous privilege.

Quietly, we shook hands. We asked Linda to take a final picture of us together. Unlike a movie plot that ultimately resolves dramatic tension, I stepped into the van overtaken by a restlessness that would linger for years. As we drove away, I glanced out the back window. I saw John standing silently, looking down.

Then traffic parted us.

Chapter 2
HAPPY BIRTHDAY!

AUGUST 2013

Linda and I were born two days apart in August 1953. We decided to celebrate our sixtieth birthdays at a woodland retreat just outside of Ottawa, Canada, for a romantic and reflective getaway. It had been twelve years since we had visited Good Samaritan orphanage.

The day I met John, he told me his heartfelt longing to become a lawyer. All through the years, John's parting words reverberated in my mind and pulled on my heart: "Please don't ever forget me." So many life experiences fade with time; John's story never did. It simply wouldn't let me go. Occasionally, I told the story, but only to my closest friends. It was a treasured moment, and I never wanted to cheapen its meaning. It didn't matter how often I reflected on it, how many times I tried to dissect and figure it out, emotion overwhelmed all powers of comprehension. Some mysteries are best left untrammeled by reason.

As I heard John grasp for opportunity, he inspired me to serve. I simply could not walk away with indifference. Within a year after returning from that trip, Linda and I became deeply engaged helping children in Kenya. Our involvement blossomed far beyond what we'd ever imagined. In 2003, Linda and I helped start an organization serving thousands of children upcountry near the city of Meru. That children's welfare operation, Ripples International, began as a rescue center for AIDS orphans. Linda also helped launch one of the first shelters in Kenya for sexually abused girls, which was later incorporated into Ripples. Eventually, an elementary school and pediatric clinic were added. From 2012 to 2018, I served as the chairman of the board of trustees. For nearly twenty years, many children benefited from our efforts and the far greater contributions of others. I recently retired from banking, but my work in Africa continues to this day.

Although we traveled to Kenya nearly every year after 2001, I never seriously tried to get back to Mathare. Reasons abounded. What taxi driver would consider taking a white man into that dangerous slum? And even if I could get a driver to take me, who would escort me down that long hill? How would I arrange for escorts to accompany me?

For too many years, I was satisfied to soak in the emotional luxury of remembering that morning with John as the source of deep inspiration for my work with other disadvantaged children in Kenya.

* * *

During our woodland retreat, I decided to write the story of the day I met John. As I composed several pages, a sense of unease came over me. Memories were no longer enough; too much lay unresolved.

After completing a draft, I showed it to Linda and told her how unsettled I felt. "What kind of story is this?" I asked, perturbed. "An American businessman spends a morning in an African slum, meets a young man, is deeply moved, comes home, helps start a children's welfare operation. It all sounds great, but where is John in all of this? He's nearly thirty years old by now. What ever happened to him? Did he become a lawyer, or did he just fade into the streets of Mathare?"

As I spoke, a bizarre thought popped into my head. "Linda, I have to find John."

Chapter 3
MARTIN, THE TAXI DRIVER

SEPTEMBER 2013

But resignation quickly crept in, and my enthusiasm for finding John slowly faded. My head told me this quest was ridiculous. In my more cynical moods, I mused to myself sarcastically, *Oh, what an admirable goal to try to find an orphan in an African shantytown, someone you haven't even talked to in twelve years! How quixotic, how melodramatic, how hopeless.*

One month after our birthday weekend, I was asked to come to Kenya on urgent business. Ripples was sponsoring a fund-raising marathon in which members of the Kenyan national team would compete. The governor and senator of Meru County (a Kenyan state) had unexpectedly accepted invitations to speak, and since I was chairman, it was now imperative that I attend as well. Linda and I had already planned to take her sister and nephews to Kenya

19

later that year, so we decided I'd travel alone.

Arranging last-minute flights meant that I'd arrive in Nairobi in the middle of the night. I had lived for five years in another tough metropolis, Mexico City, and I knew that an American businessman doesn't jump into any cab in the wee hours and blithely assume he'll be whisked to his destination. Lightning kidnappings by pirate taxi drivers were not uncommon, and Nairobi was unaffectionately known as "Nai-robbery." I inquired ahead of time to make sure I knew the location of the official taxi dispatch. I was told to go to the Kenya Airports Authority (KAA) desk just outside of the customs hall, where a dispatcher would arrange a legitimate service to drive me safely to my hotel.

I arrived from Chicago at Nairobi's Jomo Kenyatta International Airport at about 3:00 a.m. After collecting my luggage, I passed through customs and walked out to a sea of unfamiliar faces—friends and family waiting to greet loved ones and a forest of signs held by appointed drivers, but none of them for me. Looking around futilely for the KAA desk, I surely gave off the scent of an unclaimed soul, instinctively detected by taxi drivers who fell on their prey. All at once, three approached me, boasting of their first-rate services. Never wanting to make eye contact, I shooed them away, striding forward, intent on finding that KAA booth.

Finally, I spotted someone in a faded dark-blue uniform frayed around the edges. For all I know, it might have been a janitor. But at that hour anyone appearing vaguely official was good enough for me. "Madam, can you please direct me to the KAA desk? I need a taxi."

Quizzically, the uniformed public servant lazily waved across the hall to an empty metal desk emblazoned with a shiny yellow and blue KAA emblem.

A streak of desperation flashed through me. I had to give up. *All right then*, I thought, *with which of these bandits do I throw in my lot?*

As I took those last dejected steps toward the vacant desk, most drivers had turned in search of other customers. One young man, however, had persisted. A tall handsome fellow sporting a fashionable sweater and neatly pressed trousers had stayed with me the entire time. Out of options, my street smarts for naught, I crankily inquired, "So how much to take me to the Fairview Hotel?"

"That will be 2,300 shillings" ($23), "sir."

Well that was unexpectedly polite. But it only piqued my suspicions. *Remember*, I told myself, *trust no one.*

"Okay, okay," I exclaimed, by now quite annoyed and frustrated.

"There's going to be a bit of a wait," he explained. "Taxis can't park at the curb; they have to remain in another lot and then come pick up the passenger. I'll ask my friend to get the car, and we'll just have to wait for a minute."

Oh, right. A "minute" in Africa is nowhere near sixty seconds, and now there's going to be two of them and me all by myself. Oh, well, let's just get this over with. "Fine, fine," I clipped.

Waiting at the curb, I decided to strike up a conversation. If I was going to ride with a stranger at this hour, I was going to try to establish some rapport and get to know who was driving me through darkest Nairobi. We made small talk about the taxi

21

business and what it's like to work the night shift. We filled the cool moist air with idle comments about the arrival times of various air carriers. He told me that he had been on duty just a few weeks ago during the night the airport burned down. We began to joke and shared a hearty laugh about the rumor that the government had deliberately set fire to its own airport to get international aid to construct a new one.

I started to feel comfortable with the young man as his car pulled up, a shiny, light green compact station wagon. I was relieved to see that his friend turned over the wheel and would not be coming with us. As we proceeded out of the airport, I began to ask him some personal questions. I learned that he was from the Luhya tribe from Kakamega in western Kenya. He had moved here many years ago when his father brought the family to Nairobi in search of work.

"So, you've lived in Nairobi for quite a while?"

"Yes, I grew up in Mathare."

I could hardly believe what I'd heard. Mathare, he had grown up in Mathare! Could this really be true?

I paused and then asked, "Have you ever heard of the Good Samaritan orphanage?"

"Of course. Everyone in Mathare knows Good Samaritan. I lived on the other side of the river, but I passed by it every so often."

Now I had to ask, "Do you know a young man about your age named John Maina? He grew up in Good Samaritan."

"No, sir. Why do you ask?"

I explained that I had met this boy twelve years ago and wanted to find him again.

Puzzled, he asked, haltingly, "You haven't seen him in twelve years, and now you want to find him?"

I was so excited I nearly cut him off. "Son, what's your name?"

"I'm Martin," he stated with dignity.

"Martin, would it be possible for you to go to Good Samaritan and see if anyone knows anything about John? I have to be in Meru tomorrow, or I'd go with you."

"I'd be happy to, sir."

When we got to the hotel, we exchanged email addresses. Martin got a man hug and a big tip.

* * *

Two days later, in the middle of a business meeting in Meru, my Blackberry buzzed and vibrated. Yanking it out of my pocket, I was about to shut it down but first took a moment to read the incoming message. It was from Martin: "I found John Maina."

PART II
JOHN'S EARLY LIFE
—————— 1983 - 2002 ——————

To everything there is a season …
A time to be born, and a time to die …
… a time to break down, and a time to build up;
A time to weep, and a time to laugh …

—Ecclesiastes 3:1–4 (KJV)

Chapter 4
MUM AND DADDIES

John Maina was told by one of his aunts that he had been born in 1983. His mother proudly claimed that it was on December 12, the anniversary of Kenya's independence from Great Britain twenty years earlier. No certificate recorded John's birth in the Pumwani Maternity Hospital, Kenya's largest maternity clinic, principally providing services to the lower classes.

When he was three years old and again a few times when he was four, John spoke with his father. John never recalled seeing his parents together and always sensed tension in his mother's voice the few times she mentioned him. Over the years, John would come to have a better understanding of why Kenya split from its mother country than why his mother and father split from each other.

Once in a while, when he was playing in the bar where his mother worked, she would spot his father passing along the busy

Juja Road. She would point out tall, lanky James Irungu, the rumpled vendor of second-hand clothes for which he was a walking advertisement. John would catch a glimpse of him between the endless scrum of noisy *matatus* (buses) belching clouds of choking, noxious exhaust perfumed with the sweet smell of diesel.

A few times, John and his half brother, Daniel Macharia, older by two years, ran out and caught up with Irungu. Little sister, Jane, two years John's junior, was far too young to venture into the chaotic traffic.

"Hello, Irungu," the boys said with trepidation, not quite sure what reply to expect.

"Hello, Maina. Hello, Macharia," came the terse response, in typical Kenyan fashion referring to the boys by their last names. Although younger than Daniel, Irungu greeted John first since he was his natural son. Daniel was from a different father. Occasionally, the boys would shake his hand, and Irungu would quickly continue on his way. These brief encounters were the sum total of his parenting. John never felt he could call him "Daddy" because he believed a dad takes care of you each and every day. After his last encounter with his father at age four, it would be nearly three decades before John would next set eyes on Irungu.

His mother, Keziah Wanjiru, was a beautiful, slender woman with angular features and smooth, coffee-colored skin embracing a warm, loving spirit. She was born in Murang'a, a small city in fertile farm country about fifty miles north of Nairobi. From an early age, Keziah's parents sent her to school, which was unusual for a girl living in the countryside. Relations with her parents became strained however, when they refused to pay her secondary school

John's treasured photo of his mother, Keziah Wanjiru

fees, insisting she stay home to attend to domestic duties.

So, after completing Form Two (second year of high school), she left to seek employment in Nairobi. For a woman in the 1970s, she was quite successful. She started as a waitress at the Gathare Bar, a small nondescript neighborhood establishment serving a full range of drink with a butcher in the back room preparing *nyama choma* (grilled meat, usually goat). Quickly, she advanced to the role of accountant, a position of great trust in a Kenyan bar.

Many drinking establishments in Kenya are laid out with a special security feature. Unlike bars in the United States, there is no long counter with high stools where customers chat up the bartender. In fact, there's no bar counter at all. Rather, customers sit at tables. Waitresses take the orders and then repair to a metal cage behind which all liquor is kept. Although the liquor is visible to the customers, the cage is locked, and all bottles are placed against the back wall, well out of reach of aggressive patrons. The accountant is the only person inside the cage. She controls the two most valuable assets in the bar—she handles the liquor, filling orders brought by the waitresses, and she manages the cash register.

Keziah was a hard worker and well regarded by the owners of Gathare. Her working hours were from 8:00 a.m. to 11:00 p.m. After closing, she would typically arrive home before midnight. The bar's watchman would always accompany her along the several blocks to her home. Though long hours, working in a bar afforded her the benefit of being paid daily, unlike casual laborers in Kenya, who received their wages weekly, or salaried workers, who were paid monthly.

Keziah saved her money wisely, enough to rent a solid lower middle-class flat on First Street in the respectable Eastleigh community. It was one block off the Juja Road, which separated her neighborhood from Mathare, a vast gulley of poverty straddling an eponymous river choking with filth.

Keziah and her children lived in a well-kept residential area of solid cinderblock structures. Lining a wide dirt street were two- and three-story buildings, some their natural gray, others washed in faded yellow and pink hues, interspersed with low single-family dwellings and the occasional merchant's shop. What the neighborhood lacked in physical charm, it made up with its lively streets bustling with *wanachi* (common Kenyans) going about their daily lives.

Her ground-floor apartment was in a clean, six-flat structure situated behind high stone walls and an iron-gated entrance. She and the children occupied two ample bedrooms, a kitchen, bathroom, and sitting room, fully replete with electricity and running water. The live-in maid, Njeri, meticulously attended to the duties of the household. "Aunt Njeri," as the children called her, shared a room with them. They slept on comfortable bunk beds; she curled up on a mattress on the floor.

The neighborhood was alive with families, a place where children could grow up safely. Kids were always roaming about, and John could usually be found playing in the streets. Better off than most in the neighborhood, Keziah would invite her children's playmates into the apartment for a snack and sometimes even an entire lunch, a generous gesture few parents in the neighborhood could afford to extend. Always an attentive mother, Keziah would look out the window to keep an eye on her children so they wouldn't wander too far. Naturally, John sometimes disobeyed and strayed deeper into the neighborhood. When he returned, she would mete out a sound thrashing with her slipper, stiff enough to deliver a reprimand but soft enough not to cause injury.

John and Daniel occasionally played together during these early years; however, John was put off by his older brother's strong, domineering personality. The root of the tension was much deeper than prosaic sibling rivalry; it lay in their very bloodlines. Not only did John and Daniel have different fathers, John was of pure Kikuyu stock while Daniel was suspected to be a mix of Kikuyu and Luo, a potent blend of Kenya's two most powerful rival tribes. Friction between the brothers was always just below the surface, so they often went their own ways, each developing his own circle of friends.

Among her children, however, Keziah played no favorites. She would often bring little treats into their room as they were falling asleep. She would quietly push open the door, tiptoe over to the bunks, and place a warm sausage under each child's nose. What a delightful bedtime snack! Sometimes she'd bring chips or samosas; it was always a wonderful surprise.

Keziah was also an enterprising spirit. Outside the walls of the apartment complex, she erected a simple rectangular cinder block room opening onto the street. This served as a small wholesale shop dealing in an array of foodstuffs and household products, such as flour, sugar, tea leaves, and soaps.

A neat, energetic woman who exuded poise and confidence, Keziah attracted many suitors. Over time, several men lived in the flat but never stayed for more than a month or so. They brought treats to John, Daniel, and Jane—candies, milk, and even an occasional ice cream. Since these were the sorts of things John thought a father was supposed to do—provide food, buy shoes, pay school fees and the rent—he addressed each of them as "Daddy." But just as he came to know one Daddy, that man was gone.

In January 1988, when he had just turned four years old, Keziah enrolled John in kindergarten, along with Daniel. It was one of the happiest times of John's childhood. Every morning, Njeri would wake the boys at six o'clock, give them a bath, prepare tea and pack snacks for their morning break. At 7:30, she would grab their hands and walk one-quarter mile to St. Theresa's, a well regarded Catholic elementary school in Eastleigh. At lunchtime, she would return to the school and escort them home. When it was raining, she would carry them on her back, taking Daniel home first and then going back for John.

John loved school. It was fun to have so many new playmates. The teachers were kind, understanding, and attentive, like having a second set of parents. Best of all, he was not punished and had ample time to sleep when he got tired. It was exciting to be in the classroom learning about animals and letters and numbers. Walls were filled with colorful posters printed with large letters and bright numbers running from 1 to 10. For the first time, he sat at a desk with its diminutive matching chair. The schoolyard was like nothing he had ever seen, a lush lawn the size of an entire soccer field. At lunchtime, he loved to open his sack to see what Njeri had prepared. He was especially happy when he found a *mandazi* (doughnut) and a small can of milk.

John had two special kindergarten friends, Arthur Gitonga and Eunice Achieng, who sat on either side of him at their table of fifteen cohorts. Arthur was tallest in the class and always carried a football (soccer ball) in his schoolbag. At recess, he would unsheathe the ball, but he'd only play with John, his best friend. John was particularly sweet on Eunice, whom he'd meet every morning before school. She always carried biscuits and candies, which they'd count and divide and then share with Arthur.

Two teachers covered the kindergarten class at St. Theresa's, Miss Mueni and Miss Jambi. Miss Mueni mostly taught John's table; she was his favorite. She was always careful to kindly correct mistakes and was sure that no one lagged behind.

Miss Mueni also supervised PE classes and playground

activities. John's favorite game was hide-and-seek. John and Eunice had a special arrangement when they were on opposite teams; if they ever spotted each other, they promised they would never announce it to the other players.

But at the very time that John entered kindergarten, his mother began acting strangely. She started coming home later, after 1:00 a.m., and would bang loudly on the front gate. Sometimes she wouldn't come home until the following morning, when she'd hurriedly prepare breakfast for the children and immediately return to the bar.

She seemed muddled and talked peculiarly. Some neighbors said she was bewitched, a common explanation for any sort of offbeat behavior or mental disorder. Others said she was just a drunkard. Young John was confused and scared by the strange demeanor. She would frequently disappear for several hours at a stretch, returning home walking unevenly, babbling nonsensically. As time went on, the absences became longer, walking turned to a stagger, and the behavior grew more bizarre. Keziah was descending into a dark, tangled web of drunken madness, which none of the children could possibly comprehend.

While he painfully witnessed his mother's decline, John also treasured her maternal love. Even as she would wander aimlessly through Eastleigh, when she'd see her children on the street, she'd perk up, burst into tears, and give each of them a big hug. Hobbled though she was, John would remember her years later as a lovely mum.

As she spiraled ever lower, Keziah would leave the family for days at a time. When she did return home, it was usually only for a short while, just long enough to gobble down a bit of food and lift some tableware, which she'd later sell for drink. She was spotted wandering the neighborhood at all hours, stumbling, inebriated, and incoherent.

Eventually, Keziah was dismissed from her job at the Gathare Bar. The neighborhood gossip was that she supported herself by washing glasses in dark huts serving *changa'a* (moonshine). In exchange, she obtained an endless supply of 180-proof hooch.

Keziah took to sleeping in changa'a dens during weekdays. During the weekends when the bars were crowded with drunks passed out all night, she would try to find a woman to stay with. Occasionally, she'd be taken in by her sisters, Mariamu and Waiyeggo, who lived in the area. But that was not a reliable option, since Keziah was not on good terms with either one. Although she was well known throughout Mathare, her friends were also reluctant to take her in, lest she walk off with some of their possessions.

At the same time, her wholesale business faltered. Now with no source of income, beloved Njeri went unpaid until she finally had to leave the family. In May 1988, her sisters intervened and committed Keziah to the Mathare Mental Hospital, a dismal asylum across the valley just a couple miles from home.

With Keziah institutionalized, the children were left alone; the aunts stubbornly refused to help. Seeing the desperate family situation, kindly neighbors stepped in. With a magnanimous communal spirit that is so wonderfully African, they began caring for the children, providing them their daily meals. The boys were forced to drop out of school less than half a year after starting. Daniel, John, and Jane would spend their days in the apartment, only occasionally venturing outside to play.

During this time, John and Daniel first began wandering the streets at night, occasionally sleeping outside in safe nooks along the sidewalks of Eastleigh. As they became more adept at street life, they ventured across the Juja Road into the Mathare slum. There they discovered a haven, a community toilet and shower facility operated by the city council.

The enclosed structure offered several benefits. It was open all night and had a regular flow of traffic, which meant the boys were not dangerously isolated. Best of all was a strange, perhaps accidental architectural feature. Over the hallway to the men's room was a sturdy, taut four-foot-by-four-foot partial ceiling made of framed chicken wire that could support the weight of two young boys. Before going to sleep, John and Daniel would collect clean, used boxes; break them down; and lay them on the wire mesh. Once burrowed in, they were virtually undetectable at night. Besides being safe, their nest was warm, especially when they wrapped themselves in plastic sacks on cool Nairobi nights. In the morning, they'd hide their makeshift bedding on the roof, holding it in place with two large stones. Despite these many advantages, the major disadvantage of their loft hideaway was that it was directly above a rank of rancid, ill-functioning urinals.

In late 1988, Keziah was released from the hospital without a diagnosis, or at least not one that young John could comprehend. Although happy to have their mother home, the children found that her behavior was still uneven, leaving them constantly apprehensive. Restoring a normal family routine proved difficult, and finances remained precarious. Prior to her illness, Keziah had regularly paid rent six months in advance. During the time she was in the asylum, rent was covered. However, shortly after she returned, the landlord came for the next installment. The funds were not available, but that was incidental, since Keziah's behavior soon dangerously unraveled.

One night, their joyful bedtime routine took a sinister turn. Not quite asleep, John heard his mother push open the door. He eagerly anticipated a delicious treat. However, this time she was not carrying a sausage or candy. She had been cutting *ugali* (African maize polenta) and held a soiled knife. She sat on the edge of John's bed as she had done so many times. Then she reached under the covers, slowly pulled out his leg, and methodically cut a shallow two-inch incision across his lower calf. John screamed in pain. She spouted a feeble apology— "Sorry, sorry"—and told him to settle down. Immediately, she jumped over to Jane's bed and began cutting her leg as well.

With his brother and sister now screaming in pain, Daniel quickly sized up the situation. He grabbed a heavy shoe and hurled it against their mother's arm, knocking the knife from her grasp. She ran from the room, sobbing. Daniel locked the door and tended to his siblings' wounds. Since their bedroom was an interior space with no windows and thick stone walls, none of the neighbors heard their cries.

The next morning, ashamed and embarrassed, Keziah vigorously apologized to the children. To make amends, she brought them their favorite soft drink— orange Fanta—and bandaged their legs. She asked only that this incident remain a family secret.

For the next several weeks, Daniel was keenly on guard,

carefully gauging their mother's behavior. When he saw her coming home acting strangely, he feared he might be the next to have his leg cut, so he'd grab John and head for the toilet block in Mathare.

Jane was too young to accompany them onto the streets, so they had to leave her behind. To protect her from their unstable mother, the boys would padlock Jane in the flat and tell the neighbors not to allow their mother to enter under any circumstances. At dawn the next morning, John and Daniel would return and unlock the door. The neighbors would then feed the three children. For the next few weeks, the brothers alternated between accommodation in their own apartment and occasional tenants of the city council sanitary facility.

Keziah's sisters never once took in the children during her absence, but they did take advantage of their sister's incapacity. One week before the rent expired, the aunts stripped the apartment bare, removing all of the furniture and what was left of the family's smaller possessions. At the same time, the neighbors became exhausted by the burden of caring for someone else's children.

So, at the end of 1988, at the ages of five and seven years old, without a father to be found, their mother wandering the neighborhood, and facing eviction from their flat, John and Daniel decided to take to the streets. Since their little sister was too young and the neighborhoods too dangerous, they appealed to a kindly old woman, Mrs. Wairimu, one of Keziah's friends, who took pity on the children's situation. She gladly accepted three-year-old Jane into her home. Once they knew their sister was in good hands, the two boys abandoned the empty flat to live on the streets of Eastleigh.

Three years after this picture was taken, Daniel (left) and John (right) would be on the streets and Jane would be living with a neighbor.

Chapter 5
GITARI

After leaving the apartment, John and Daniel drifted into the commercial center of Eastleigh. Although they had made some forays onto the streets, they had always been able to return to their apartment, but that refuge was no longer available. They were now truly street boys.

They wandered up 1st Avenue, intimidated by tall four- and five-story buildings. Streets were buzzing with activity and packed with shoppers. Open storefronts displayed their wares spilling onto the sidewalks—clothing of all descriptions, both Western styles and long, flowing Muslim garb, handbags and backpacks, electronic devices, audio systems blaring to attract attention. Traffic snarled to a stop. John and Daniel were swallowed in a morass of humanity, commerce, and vehicles.

Turning the corner at Galole Street, only about five blocks

from their apartment, John saw an older boy sitting by himself on the sidewalk sniffing glue. John thought the boy might be able to assist, so he approached. Daniel remained at a distance. Exuding a good-natured geniality, the older boy introduced himself as "Gitari." He could see that John and Daniel were together but was puzzled by Daniel's hesitance. Finally, John introduced his brother.

Seeing the two disoriented by the chaotic street, Gitari asked them to sit down. John and Gitari exchanged stories about their backgrounds. Daniel barely spoke. John learned that Gitari was eleven years old and, like their mother, was from Murang'a. He had left home because his parents were always drunk, and his grandparents were never around. So, four years ago, at the age of seven, he had walked fifty miles to Nairobi on his polio-afflicted leg in search of his uncles who supposedly lived in the city. Unable to locate them, he had been on the streets ever since.

John explained that he and Daniel had left their home just a few hours ago and now had to make their way on the streets. As dusk was settling over the city, Gitari invited them to join him at his base on a strip of sidewalk in front of a dealer of Eveready batteries half a block down Galole Street. The proprietor was happy to have someone out front at night, since their presence offered a modicum of security for the store. He insisted, however, that their bedding be cleared, and the walk swept early every morning before customers arrived.

Although veterans of many nights at the city council toilet block, John and Daniel had never slept outside along a busy street. Gitari pulled several dusty, flattened cardboard boxes and three filthy sacks from the roof of the low building next to his base. This was their bedding. That night, John slept poorly. He was accustomed to the clean boxes and shiny plastic wraps he and Daniel had used in their loft. He was also used to the relative quiet of the toilet block. Across the street from the base, though, was a raucous club with loud music and bawdy clientele. All about was the persistent hum of the city. Huddled together in their loft, John and Daniel used to keep each other warm. However, on the open street and concrete sidewalk, they were cold to the bone. John slept, as best he could, sitting up the entire night. The second night was not much better. But by the third, John had become accustomed to the conditions and slept supine through to the next morning.

John and Gitari quickly became friends. Daniel saw that Gitari knew the streets well and could provide leadership and authority, which he could not. In no position to satisfy his domineering personality but needing the guidance Gitari provided, Daniel stayed at the base at night but went his own way during the day.

On every one of Eastleigh's cross streets, from 1st through 12th, boys formed into groups. Sleeping and eating were highly territorial for street boys. One of Gitari's main responsibilities as leader of his street family was to ensure the safety and cohesion of the members of his band. If a new boy showed up and professed interest in joining, Gitari would conduct extensive due diligence to determine the young man's background. Over time, Gitari came to know virtually every street boy in Eastleigh. He was a cool operator and was never known to aggressively harass anyone. On more than one occasion, his savvy and street smarts thwarted attempted infiltration into his group by a rival gang.

Not long after John and Daniel joined Gitari, several others came along. The fourth member of the band was a boy named Mouo, who took to the streets at about the same time as John and Daniel. Mouo had stayed with his single mother, who had served as a live-in maid for a Hindu family in a nearby slum. When the family returned to India, Mouo's mother was let go and had to make her own way. In time, she remarried, but the stepfather did not like Mouo, who eventually left home because of the constant mistreatment he received. One of the most common reasons for taking to the streets was the friction between children and their stepparents, who felt little responsibility and often animosity for those not their blood kin. Occasionally, Mouo's mother would come looking for him on the streets and bring him home. Invariably, after about a week though, Mouo was back at the base.

Soon after Mouo joined, Gitari allowed Vincent Ochieng and Steven Kivindu into the group. Vincent's family hailed from the western province of Nyanza, which means "lake" since it borders the shores of Lake Victoria. Like so many others, the family moved to Nairobi in search of work. Unfortunately, shortly after arriving in the city, Vincent's father died. His mother took his sister, Pinta Auma, to Eastleigh where they supported themselves by providing domestic services. But they were unable to support Vincent, and he was forced onto the streets, eventually making his way to Galole Street and Gitari's band. Vincent was a reserved boy, so quiet he rarely conversed at all. He never bullied others and, thus, gave off the pervasive air of a withdrawn, contemplative child.

Steven Kivindu was a large boy with dark-black complexion. He was an intimidating youth, muscular with a booming voice for his age. He left home because his drunken father repeatedly abused his mother. To defend himself in his violent home, Steven took up boxing. On the streets, he became the bodyguard and enforcer for the group. So imposing was his presence that, in an altercation, he would step out front, emit a thunderous roar, and rival gangs would scatter.

Gitari's band was never more than this handful of boys, all under twelve years old. John soon became his deputy. He saw that, besides protecting his own, Gitari was an individual of high integrity. Gitari knew too well that the street may be the only alternative to an abusive home life, but he also knew that some runaways were spoilt upstarts acting out. After extensive questioning, if he felt a boy had run away from a good home, he would seek out the parents and return their prodigal son. Without doubt, Gitari was one of the all-time good guys on the street.

Chapter 6
PLASTIC, METALS, AND BONES

In 1989, John's first full year on the streets, UNICEF estimated that 100 million children around the world were living in similar conditions.[1] The overwhelming majority were boys between the ages of eleven and fifteen, living mostly in Latin America, Asia, and Africa. About 25 percent were girls.[2]

Gathering recyclable plastic and metal scraps was one of the most common means of surviving on the streets. Children also gathered animal bones, which were later ground up to make ceramic ware. Street boys would often rise at dawn, grab their gunnysacks—discarded packaging for ninety kilos of bulk grains—and comb the streets collecting these materials. Bigger, stronger boys wouldn't scrounge for tiny scraps; they'd hang out near auto repair shops

[1] Consortium for Street Children, Briefing Paper, 2015
(www.streetchildren.org/about-street-children)
[2] Smile Foundation Kenya, Statistics (www.smilefoundationkenya.com)

47

waiting to carry off large disused vehicle parts. Sometimes, they'd walk the railroad tracks searching for heavy lug nuts and loose tie plates.

Because the city council was always strapped for funds, garbage wasn't regularly picked up for the millions who lived in Nairobi's shantytowns. Enterprising souls dealt with the community's taka-taka (refuse) by establishing dumps in various open tracts in the slums. The pungent aroma of the sweet decay of rotting food filled the air around these sites. Sprawling eight-foot high pyramids of newly delivered waste were checkered with black and bright green plastic bags commonly used in Kenya. Men and women carefully picked through the mound, looking for the same materials street boys hunted daily. They separated organic matter to sell as slop for pigs. Wading up to the rims of their gumboots in refuse, these workers were proud of their occupation and disdained being referred to as chokara meaning "filthy person," a derogatory name for garbage pickers and a common insult for street boys. Rather, theirs was an honorable service to the community, which indeed it was, given the city council's abject neglect.

The site John frequented was at the dead end of a street terminating against the outer wall of the Moi Air Force Base on the eastern edge of Eastleigh. When he and his fellow street boys had collected all the scraps they could find, they would make their way to the dump to sell their haul. For street boys, this was a key port of call in their daily survival routine. Going rates at the time John was on the streets were:

Plastic containers 5 shillings (5 cents)/kilo[3]
Metals   10 shillings (10 cents)/kilo
Bones   2 shillings (2 cents)/kilo

At the edge of the garbage mound was a small structure, nothing more than a flat crooked roof uneasily propped on four posts. Hanging from a crossbeam was the weighing machine, simply a hook coming off a scale face, much like those in grocery stores.

Since the operators of the weigh stations didn't carefully check the quality and condition of the scraps, devious boys would fill some of the bottles with water to increase the weight. The work was tiring, and John usually napped against the sloping garbage mounds after a long morning of scavenging.

On the streets, boys often acquired nicknames. John's was "Mdudu," which means "worm." In the United States, calling someone worm would be a serious put-down, but not in Eastleigh and not for the reason John earned it.

John was an industrious five-year-old street dweller. The typical nightly routine for the boys was to assemble at their base around 10:00 p.m., spread out their boxes and sacks on the sidewalk, smoke some bhang (marijuana) to relax, and be asleep by eleven o'clock. Most boys would wake between 5:00 and 6:00 a.m. to begin collecting scraps. Some nights, John would tell everyone he planned to sleep until 7:00 a.m. Others scoffed at his apparent laziness. At 3:00 a.m., however, John would rise carefully, quietly take his sack, and get cracking.

Since he didn't have a watch or any instrument he could set

---

[3] Throughout the book, 1 Kenyan shilling equals 1 US cent; 100 shillings equal US$ 1

as an alarm, John relied on the late-night matatus to wake him up. Each morning at one o'clock, one of these buses would blow its horn as it passed nearby; that was his first wake-up call. Between 2:30 and 3:00 a.m. at the shift change for night workers, the next matatu would announce its arrival. When this second horn blared, John knew it was time to get up. If one of his cronies happened to wake as John was leaving, he'd give the excuse that he was going for "a long call" (in other words, to defecate). They'd go back to sleep, and John would be on his way.

There was a method to his early-morning forays. While the others were still sleeping, John would comb every road from 6th Street up to 12th Street, gathering all sorts of materials. Plastics were easy to find, since discarded water bottles were ubiquitous. The big payoff was finding metals and large quantities of bone. John discovered that the best place to look for metals was outside each home in the small firepits in which residents cooked their meals. Wood was the principal fuel used for cooking, most of which was salvaged from construction site waste, which contained metal fasteners—nails, screws, and bolts. By early morning when the embers had cooled, John could sift through the ashes or use a "spark" (magnet) to retrieve the metal scraps.

Although bones paid little per kilo, it was a boon to find a reliable source of large quantities. In his predawn jaunts, John came across a butcher who, in the wee hours, routinely dressed animals for his daily display. After cultivating a cordial relationship, John offered to carry water to the butcher in exchange for the fileted carcasses. With the mutual agreement sealed by a handshake, John would time his early morning excursions to arrive at the butchery at about five o'clock.

By dawn, having thoroughly scoured the vicinity before his comrades awoke, John would hide his bulging sack on a nearby rooftop and crawl back onto his cardboard mattress, pretending to be asleep. Just like a worm that is silent and eats quietly, John was a very successful "worm," quietly going about his business while the world rested.

Eventually, some of the boys caught onto John's game and asked to join him in an early start. On several occasions, two or three boys woke with John well before dawn to learn his ways. Unwilling to divulge his valuable secrets, however, John would send them down routes he knew would be fruitless. Furthermore, he had no intention of letting on his technique with the spark. Nor would he introduce them to the butcher. Tired and discouraged, the others quickly gave up and ceded those small hours to Mdudu.

* * *

As Gitari's band became more accustomed to the neighborhood around their base, they were "adopted" by prostitutes who plied their trade across the street from their base at a bar appropriately named Tupedane ("Let's love one another"). Eventually the boys and the hookers set up a mutual protection arrangement. Since the boys were still quite young, the ladies felt a maternal inclination to watch over them. But the ladies themselves needed assistance from time to time. Now and then, a client would shortchange a girl after services had been performed. As the man attempted to slink away, the ladies would shout to the boys, who would pelt the john with stones until he paid up.

In addition to establishing safe sleeping quarters, the other main domestic matter was to secure a consistent source of food. Just a few doors from the Eveready shop was the Shamshudin Hotel. A hotel in Kenya does not have the same meaning as it does in the United States, where a hotel is an establishment offering sleeping accommodation. Hotels in Kenya function as eateries, and there is a broad range of quality—from large, clean, well-appointed restaurants offering a full-scale menu to tiny shanties made of scrap lumber with a couple of chairs serving tea and bread to poor casual laborers trudging their way to work in the morning.

"Taking tea" is a Kenyan expression that often confuses Americans. In the United States, tea is a drink often consumed by itself at any time of the day. Although Kenyans also drink tea at any time of the day, "taking tea" means eating breakfast. This morning meal for Kenyans consists of a drink (tea or porridge), along with bread, biscuits, or a fried dough pastry.

The Shamshudin was an upscale establishment catering to well-to-do Somalis, who were a large minority in Eastleigh. The Eastleigh district of Nairobi is known as "Little Mogadishu," taking its nickname from the capital and largest city of Somalia. Eastleigh is a bustling commercial quarter with a wide array of shops owned by Somalis, who are famous for their business acumen.

Unlike American restaurants, which have dumpsters at the back door, in Kenya food waste often must be hauled to the nearest refuse tip. These might be several hundred yards away. In the same manner that street boys marked their sleeping quarters, they would also mark their hotels. Each morning, the squad of boys favored by the hotel would show up at the back door at the time designated by the kitchen staff where they'd be given buckets of waste from the previous day. Sometimes the buckets were heavy, and two or three boys would be needed to handle the load. For their services, the kitchen staff manager would pay fifty shillings after the bucket was returned within the hour.

Clearly the money was welcomed, but the collateral benefit of linking up with a hotel was the opportunity to rummage through the buckets for food. Carrying the bucket on the way to the dump, John and his companions would pause en route to pick through the waste. They'd lay out several plastic shopping bags and begin sorting. One pile was for obvious garbage, such as cigarette butts, tissue paper, toothpicks, and bottle caps. As they came across leftovers, they would inspect the scraps to determine if these were still edible and, if so, divide the trove among the team. A boy could only eat if he helped carry the buckets. John and his comrades ate from the Shamshudin each morning and evening.

Sometimes the leftovers were of such high quality that the boys would set them aside for resale. These were usually chicken and fine sausages that had been prepared in advance by the kitchen but had not been ordered by the previous day's clientele. Scrap food was usually heavier starches—chapati (a Kenyan tortilla), ugali, and githeri (beans and maize). Mixed in would also be the lighter foods preferred by the Somalis—spaghetti, boiled meats, lemons, bananas, and eggs.

Daniel didn't work the Shamshudin every day like most of Gitari's band. He'd usually assist two or three times each week and share the food, but because he didn't regularly carry the buckets, he wouldn't get the tip from the kitchen staff. Daniel acquired his nickname Kalulu ("Joker"), because of the way he always made others laugh. His banter, however, was calculated to be displayed only at mealtime. When boys were gathered around their castoff scraps, Daniel would put everyone in stitches, distracting them just long enough from their food to allow him to scarf a few extra bites.

The principal objectives of street boys were quite simple—establish a safe place to sleep; obtain a steady, reliable source of food; and raise enough money to buy drugs. Since street boys can sleep for free and eat for free, the only money they needed were a few shillings to keep them high. Getting bhang and glue was what propelled them to look for the scrap plastics and metals. A typical day's haul of materials would yield about 100 shillings, which would be ample to stoke one's bottle with fresh glue or buy some bhang.

The most common drug for young street boys was glue. Older boys were partial to illegal alcohol. Cocaine and heroin were available, although relatively expensive so not often taken. Industrial glue that was used to bind shoe soles to uppers was the preferred intoxicant. A boy typically hung a wide-mouthed, flask-shaped plastic bottle around his neck. Protruding from the bottle was a stick, which was used to stir the glue to prevent it from forming a skin at the surface, which would block the flow of fumes. A one-inch fill would cost twenty to fifty shillings and would suffice for half a day. The boy would raise the bottle to his nose and mouth and inhale vigorously, providing a strong, brief high. He learned not to leave the bottle in place because continuous sniffing could cause nausea or even blackout. It was critical never to fall asleep with the bottle at his mouth because the glue could run down his throat, quickly congeal, and seal his windpipe. Besides the terrific high, glue also numbed the senses, suppressing hunger pangs and dulling the skin, thus helping the boy tolerate cold weather. The downside of persistent glue sniffing was that it rotted the brain, initially manifest by slow, stammering speech.

Immediately after landing on the street, Gitari introduced John to glue. At first, he was reluctant to try. John knew about glue but had never tried it because he believed it would be bad for his health. But after a few cold nights on the streets, Gitari convinced him of the benefits. Over the course of one week, Gitari taught him the proper sniffing techniques. Initially, John thought it smelled bad and tasted bad. But by the second week, he was an expert.

Daniel did not take well to glue. During the first week of sniffing, he became so dizzy that Gitari had to take him to a children's clinic that offered free services for the poor. His good fortune was never to take glue again.

Street boys throughout Eastleigh obtained their glue through Mrs. Mutheu, an old lady who they called Sho Sho (Grandmother). A calloused old woman who fed young boys' addictions, she was known to be so tough that she would smoke cigarettes with the lit end in her mouth and swallow the ash. Amazed at the feat, John tried it once but burnt the roof of his mouth so badly that he never tried it again. She lived in a ramshackle wooden room close to St. Theresa's school. Twice a day, at about 8:00 a.m. and 6:00 p.m., John would swing by her house for a fresh fix. His financial planning required that he end each day with at least fifty shillings in his pocket so he would be able to purchase glue in the morning. When he was particularly flush with cash and Gitari would be short, John would buy him a ration of glue. Among street boys, this was a true mark of friendship.

For nearly three years, from the end of 1988 until August 1991, John and Daniel were part of Gitari's band, operating in an area about ten square blocks in the center of Eastleigh. One morning, when John and Daniel were gathering scraps, they encountered a bubbly young boy about four years old who asked if they wanted to play. Meeting Simon Mwangi would be one of the great turning points in their lives.

Chapter 7
SLEEPING SACK

Mrs. Wairimu, the gracious old lady who cared for Jane, lived in Mathare along the main road on the south side of the river. A widow with little means of support, she used to process and sell chicken scraps discarded by butchers—heads, feet, gizzards and intestines. These cheap foodstuffs were particularly desired by poor casual laborers who too often squandered most of their money on drink. Jane would earn her keep by hauling firewood and water to assist in the preparation of the delectables.

There weren't many street boys in Mathare because the neighborhood was too poor. Scraps wouldn't lie around for the boys to pick up as they did in the relatively better off Eastleigh district. Residents of Mathare would save their own materials to bring to the dumps to earn a few extra shillings. The only place in Mathare for agile street boys to collect metals and plastics was in the river.

After the first night sleeping at the base, Gitari introduced John and Daniel to the daily routine of gathering materials. At first, the brothers worked together. However, within a week, they split and went their own ways. John felt his brother's heavy hand, as Daniel insisted that John turn over everything he collected. The only time they moved about together was when they went into Mathare to visit Jane and scour the river for materials.

Jane was always thrilled to see her older brothers. Often, they would meet her along the road and help her carry water or wood to Mrs. Wairimu. When they could, they would give the widow a two- or five-shilling coin, a small contribution toward Jane's support. After visiting their sister, they'd careen down the steep slopes to the river. The best places to look for scraps were in the deep pools where metal would sink. Although only about twenty feet wide, the current could be strong and the water filthy, so precautions were necessary. It was essential for boys to wear sturdy shoes with thick soles lest they cut their feet, which would invariably result in serious infection. John would tie a rope to a tree on the bank and slowly wade into a pool. Then he'd carefully lower his spark into the foul broth to retrieve the metal treasures.

As they made their occasional rounds through Mathare, John and Daniel frequently saw a young boy playing alone in front of his home on the main street. Simon Mwangi was about four years old, a few years younger than John and not yet in school. He was the son of Mercy and James Thuo, two of the relatively more prosperous inhabitants of the slum. James was a truck driver, and Mercy a wholesaler of cereals.

James was thirty-seven years old, and Mercy was thirty-two.

For many years, they had lived in Eastleigh in a rented flat on the ground floor of a solid stone building not far from the dump site where John brought his bulging sack of materials. Several years earlier, Thuo's brother, the mayor of the neighboring municipality of Dandora, had used his connections to obtain a small tract of land in Mathare measuring fifty feet by a hundred feet. It was hardly a choice property, adjacent to a putrid septic field buzzing with mosquitos, but it was land James and Mercy could call their own, so they gladly accepted the offer.

Since land tenure was dubious and title deeds were often of little value in Kenya, especially in the slums, the best way to secure one's property was to build on it immediately, which effectively established one's rights. So, Thuo and Mercy quickly erected a small rectangular wooden structure about ten feet by thirty feet in size with three rooms—a combination kitchen / sitting room, a bedroom for themselves, and one for Simon and his two older sisters. Several rental rooms were added alongside their house to provide extra cash income. A small open-air chicken coop was built out back.

One day in August 1990, Simon approached John and Daniel and invited them to play. As young boys, they were always up for kickball, tag, or just chasing around. Simon was a slow, chubby, cheerful lad, to whom John took an immediate liking.

In time, John and his brother made sure to swing regularly through Simon's neighborhood. If their bags were full, they would stop and play. Eventually, Simon asked them to come to his house for some food. What a fantastic surprise—freshly cooked food! And better yet, there were some of their favorites that Njeri used to prepare—chicken with rice, chapati and beans, and githeri. Simon would bring a heaping plate out to the street and gladly share. John and Daniel would voraciously devour whatever was offered, much faster than Simon could get to his portion. Simon would then go back in the house crying for more, complaining that he was still hungry. Mercy would take care of him, but her curiosity was piqued. Why was he still hungry after she had served him a full plate?

As Simon became friendlier with John and Daniel, he decided to follow them deeper into the slums. For the next three months, Simon would sneak away from his home and follow the boys, helping them search for materials. He was excited to be able to assist his older friends, often shouting, "Maich! Maich" (nickname for Maina). "Come here. Look what I found!"

One day when he returned, Mercy was furious. "What are you doing wandering away from home? And why are you hanging around those filthy chokara?"

But Simon had made two friends, his only two friends, and he was not to be dissuaded. For the next year, he continued to play with the boys as they made their rounds.

Like so many parents, Mercy eventually accommodated herself to her child's wishes. However, rather than allow Simon to wander the unsafe streets of Mathare with his pals, in August 1991, she invited John and Daniel to come and live with them. This was not only to keep Simon safely nearby but because she had developed a soft spot in her heart for them. Mercy had heard from some neighbors the sad story of the two boys and their mother and realized that she had occasionally seen Keziah wandering the streets.

But Mercy's invitation wasn't exactly what John and Daniel expected. Rather than allow the boys to share Simon's room inside their home, Mercy situated the two in the chicken coop behind the house. The coop was only five-feet-by-five-feet, with flimsy walls and a roof of corrugated metal. The modest structure held three hens and a cock. The floor was packed dirt, and the four birds propagated a horrendous odor. But after sleeping on a cold sidewalk along a noisy street filled with drunks and prostitutes, this was luxurious.

There was an additional wrinkle to Mercy's offer, though. Still somewhat suspicious of the two street boys, she was concerned for her chickens. Since there was no door on the coop, she feared that the boys might carry them off during the night and sell them for their next day's ration of bread, glue, and bhang. So, the first night the boys were invited to sleep in the coop, she produced two large sacks. Excited, John thought these might serve as blankets or pillows, neither of which he had enjoyed at their base on Galole Street. But Mercy had other plans. When bedtime came, she ordered the boys into the sacks. Initially apprehensive, they both eventually agreed to crawl in. But John voiced one condition—he insisted that he take his glue bottle with him. This was critical not only to feed his addiction; the fumes also served to counteract the stench of the chicken droppings. The whole arrangement seemed strange, but he had his limits—if he couldn't keep his glue, they wouldn't stay. Since Mercy's scheme was designed to keep Simon's playmates nearby, she relented. The boys crawled into the sacks, and she tied the opening. Simon stood by, making sure they weren't tied too tightly. As she wrapped the boys up, Mercy sternly explained she wanted to make sure they didn't steal her chickens. Then she wished them a good night.

Not at all claustrophobic, John was comforted by the warmth of the sack. Besides, he didn't think Mercy understood that, if they really wanted to get out, they could easily have cut through the bags.

In the morning, Mercy would go out to the chicken coop and untie the sacks. Occasionally, she would feed them some porridge, but usually they were left to fend for themselves, returning in the late afternoon to play with Simon and crawl back into the sacks at night.

Chapter 8
GOOD SAMARITAN

When John and Daniel were on the streets of Eastleigh, they would occasionally see wealthy Somalis escorting their children to school. The boys would wistfully think back on the mornings Njeri used to walk them to St. Theresa's. John would ask his brother, "Do you think we'll ever be able to go to school again?"

"No, not just now," Daniel would reply. "We couldn't collect enough scrap materials to pay school fees or buy uniforms. Besides how would we eat? We'd be in school when all our buddies would be carrying buckets for the hotels." Then he'd pause. "But maybe someday something will work out."

* * *

Mercy saw that Simon was happy with his two playmates living on the premises, so she asked John and Daniel to bring more friends. They went back to their base and rounded up three of their best buddies—Gitari, Mouo, and Steven Kivindu. At first, the three liked receiving porridge in the morning, along with a cup of water to wash their faces. But after two days, they stopped coming. They quickly tired of the routine, the loss of freedom they enjoyed on the streets, and being literally cooped up. They also claimed they could eat better from the Shamshudin. Sadly, for John, his best friends returned to Eastleigh.

Others saw the advantages of secure sleeping quarters and a spot of breakfast. Through the first few months of 1992, ten other boys joined Mercy's chicken coop brigade, including Vincent Ochieng from Gitari's band.

One of John's casual acquaintances from the streets also came along. Peter Musyoki was the only boy in a family of three sisters. After his father died, the uncles seized their brother's patrimony and left the widow with nothing—sadly, a rather common occurrence in rural Kenya. The mother took her brood of four to Nairobi and found her way to Mathare, where she set up a small kiosk selling vegetables. To relieve his mother of the burden of caring for another hungry child, Peter went to the streets. John ran into him almost every day, usually as they were making their rounds collecting materials or at Sho Sho's room topping up their glue. Because Peter's gang wasn't well-organized, they had not marked out a hotel to eat as Gitari had laid claim to the Shamshudin for his group. Occasionally, John would invite Peter to share a meal. When Peter heard rumors that Mercy was taking in street boys, he jumped at the opportunity and found his way to her home.

With the live-in crew growing, Mercy decided to set a door for the coop to protect her chickens. She also erected a few new

Mama Mercy

makeshift walls to form a small room for the boys. Much as Simon wanted to live with the boys, Mercy insisted that he sleep inside the flat with the family.

Neighborhood donors began to support Mercy's budding charity. A lady down the street contributed two mattresses, on which all ten young boys slept, covering themselves with two threadbare blankets. As time went on, Mercy began to prepare food, which attracted more street children, but only ten chose to stay on the premises. Others in the community started contributing basic supplies—maize flour, cooking fat, rice, and sugar. Mercy knew she needed to be transparent about donations, so she appointed Peter Musyoki to the role of head boy and gave him the task of tracking all contributions. In addition to this basic oversight responsibility, Peter was also entrusted with maintaining discipline among the children.

Some locals volunteered to teach. After nearly four years without any instruction, something finally did work out for John and Daniel; they were back in school, of a sort. They learned the alphabet and mastered the distinction between vowels and consonants. The children practiced basic spelling and how to write their names. Soon they could count to one hundred and recite the days of the week and the months of the year.

As a gesture of appreciation, Mercy would give small quantities of milk to the donors and volunteers. She kept a scrawny cow behind a nearby beer den. It produced so little milk that it couldn't be used for the children's daily needs but provided enough to thank her supporters.

Toward the end of 1992, Mercy decided to bring in even more children. Most of the boys under her care had sisters who were also living without parents. The first girl to join was Jane, happily reunited with her brothers. Peter Musyoki brought his three sisters—Anna, Elisa, and Mary. Vincent convinced his sister, Pinta Auma, to move in.

By the end of 1992, twelve girls had joined Mama Mercy. This meant that the premises needed to expand once again. The girls assumed the location where the boys had slept, next to the chicken coop and directly outside the doorway to Mercy's flat. The boys were moved further away, with a small classroom set up between them and the girls' room. Now there were twenty-two children living alongside Mercy's flat. It was a great relief to the boys to have their sisters in safe quarters.

Girls generally didn't live on the streets the way boys did. Typically, after doing a day's work, a group of girls would use their earnings to purchase a shared room for the night. Some would earn money by washing clothes or cleaning houses; some would sell their bodies—not uncommon for girls as young as twelve years old. If a girl had younger siblings in her care, she could quickly make 100 shillings turning a trick, enough to buy three plates of food.

Sexual gratification was readily available for street boys. Prostitutes, of course, were unaffordable for young men barely scratching out an existence. These ladies were perceived to be fancy professionals who lived in fine quarters, plied their trade in upscale bars, and performed their services in well-appointed rooms at premium prices. Many street girls made their living through prostitution, however, without any of the supposed glamor. These young ladies were quickly identified by housewives in the community and were deemed to be too dirty, unreliable, and indecent to be hired into the home to perform domestic chores.

These girls, known as "grasshoppers," earned the nickname by jumping from boy to boy. They'd work the streets both day and night. A hookup during the day would usually take place in a narrow crevice between buildings. At night, a pair might seek privacy at the unoccupied local dump site, which only operated in daylight hours. Services would typically cost 50 to 100 shillings. If the girl happened on a group of street boys when they were eating, the charge would be a plate of food.

Although AIDS was rampant throughout Kenya in the '90s and '00s, few street boys used condoms. At that time, condoms were not freely available. Rather, they cost as much as 50 shillings for a three-pack. Such an expenditure was far beyond the budget of a boy who might only be able to scrounge together 100 shillings per day, most of which would go for drugs. Moreover, girls who desperately needed the money understood that they could not insist that their partners wear unaffordable prophylactics.

As AIDS spread, however, street boys began to fashion homemade condoms. In preparation for a tryst, a street boy would go to a nearby vegetable stand and purchase a few tomatoes or onions, which would be packed in a plastic bag. The boy would use the bag as a surrogate condom, applying lubricant to enhance the sensation.

But fatalism and hopelessness eroded the psyches of most street children, both boys and girls. After only a little while on the streets, they felt like the walking dead, without lives or any hope in their hearts. So, most sexual activities were reckless, unprotected encounters.

* * *

As Mercy's home grew from two to ten to twenty-two, John enjoyed having more children around. Not only did he have more playmates; the new arrivals were interesting and different, since they came from other Kenyan tribes, especially Luos and Kambas, in addition to his own Kikuyu lineage. The only downside to the growing population was that food portions had to be reduced to spread across more children.

But the most wonderful benefit to the expanding population was that John met Margaret Muthoni, who became his girlfriend. He was attracted to her kind disposition and her pretty, smooth chocolate complexion. Margaret and her brother, Victor Maregwa, joined Good Samaritan in 1993 after their mother died of AIDS. Mama Mercy had appointed John to be the person in charge of welcoming new arrivals, showing them the compound and explaining the rules and routines. Margaret was two years younger than John when she entered. Although only eight and ten years old at the time, they took to each other immediately. All through primary school, they enjoyed a puppy love. Margaret looked up to John as a leader to whom she could bring her concerns. He helped her get extra servings of food at dinner when she was still hungry, and he reported to Mama Mercy the older girls who were bullying Margaret in the dormitory. John and Margaret were inseparable, and everyone knew them as an item.

* * *

With a growing retinue of young souls whom she was raising under strained conditions, Mama Mercy needed to be a loving but strict matron. Weekends were time for chores. Mercy arranged for children to rotate tasks from week to week. The most involved task was washing clothes. Each Saturday, five boys and five girls would do laundry for the entire compound. They would form a line, some washing, some rinsing, others hanging. To pass the time, they would take turns singing songs. The child at the first bucket would start, and everyone would join in. Then it was the second bucket's turn and down the line of five. For three hours every Saturday morning, the children would fill the air with songs in Swahili, Luo, Kamba, and English. Although those singing in different mother tongues couldn't understand the words, they learned the pronunciations and had a grand time. The only restriction Mama Mercy put on the washing crew was that they could only sing Gospel songs. She insisted on raising the children in a Christian manner as best she could.

While wash was being done, others would sweep the compound, and another team would air out the mattresses by hauling them onto the roof. John's favorite task was raking the street-side gutters. His least favorite chore was kitchen duty, because the cooking oil would always splatter and burn his hands.

Although the home was growing in size, it was a happenstance discovery across the street that propelled Mercy's operation from its meager beginnings to citywide prominence.

* * *

Across the main road, directly opposite Mama Mercy's compound, was a steep embankment that dropped precipitously some twenty-five feet into the Mathare River. Bordering the road was a lip of ground covered with thick bushes running up to the edge of the sheer drop.

Mercy didn't have a latrine on the premises, so the children would have to walk across the street to relieve themselves in the bushes. Acrobatic and daring boys would often hold onto a sturdy bush, swing their butts over the edge, and evacuate directly into the river below.

One afternoon, John and a friend, Charles Chalo, were making their way through the bushes when they came upon a wallet and clutch of documents on the ground. The boys recognized a Barclays Bank logo. Overcoming their initial urge to use them to wipe their bums, they suspected these were important papers. After performing their intended duty, they gathered the items and brought them to Mama Mercy. Upon inspection, she quickly surmised that a Barclays Bank manager had been robbed, his money taken, and the papers, useless to the thief, had been tossed into the bushes. Mercy felt the obligation to return the documents to the manager. However, she paused cautiously. She knew that, if she or one of the older children returned them to the branch, they would be suspected of conducting the robbery and then pandering for a reward. So, Mercy told John and Charles that, since they found the papers, they should be the ones to return them.

Mercy composed a short letter to the manager informing him of the boys' discovery and proposed that he meet them at her home to retrieve his documents. One week later, a well-dressed gentleman with a pronounced limp presented himself at Mercy's door, introducing himself as a Barclays branch manager. Mercy sent for John and Charles, who proudly explained their fortuitous discovery as well as their fateful decision not to clean themselves with his papers.

Grateful that they had stayed their hands, the manager accepted his wallet and documents and presented rewards to each boy—crisp two hundred-shilling notes ($2), the largest, cleanest bill John had ever held.

Mercy registered her thanks and showed him the humble quarters she managed for children she had taken from the streets. Impressed by her honesty and generosity, the manager returned to work and began spreading the word about "this place in Mathare that takes care of orphans." Shortly thereafter, a load of foodstuffs was delivered to Mercy's home, compliments of Barclays Bank.

With the operation growing and resources steadily arriving, Mercy quit her wholesaling business to focus on the children. Her good heart, practical bent, and street smarts allowed her to support herself from the orphanage.

At about the same time, James Thuo, Mama Mercy's husband, was fired from his driver's job, having been caught DUI one too many times. Although James had not completed elementary school and clearly had a drinking problem, he provided children in the home with a strong paternal example. He was usually found sitting on a chair at the street-side entrance watching the children's comings and goings and protecting the home from unwanted intruders. Every day when the children arrived from school, he'd be in his chair at the front gate, making sure they dropped off their books and changed out of their uniforms. After dinner, he'd supervise their homework as the children crowded around a few candles, the only illumination in Good Samaritan.

He was a strict but fair disciplinarian, instilling good morals and a sense of right and wrong. As boys matured, he'd take them aside in small groups and teach basic sex education. Beyond the anatomical rudiments, Thuo would also instruct the boys in the gentlemanly behavior of how to treat a lady. Because he was such a kind, understanding, and supportive man, the children gave him the nickname "Buddha."

* * *

As word about Mercy's home was spread by the Barclays staff, other premier institutions from the Nairobi community began making their way to Mathare. Soon, there wasn't a day without visitors passing through the home. Everyone could see that Mercy was a loving matron. If it weren't for her, none of the children would have a home. Nor would they receive any schooling. Some might even be dead. Students from the prestigious University of Nairobi and Kenyatta University came to play with the children. A host of churches contributed foodstuffs. Rotary Club donated beds, Charity Sweepstakes gave mattresses, and Barclays donated blankets.

But Mercy's home still did not have a name other than "this place in Mathare." Barclays began referring to her as "the good shepherd." Students from Kenyatta University called her "the good Samaritan," which more and more visitors began to adopt.

While the neighbors were delighted to help Mercy support the children from the streets, one day John overheard a lady admonishing Mercy, "It's great that you're giving them food and shelter, but you're just keeping them here like cattle. Shouldn't they be going to a proper school?"

So, Mercy decided to approach several schools in the area to see if arrangements could be made to enroll some of the children. But how would she present herself and her home? She settled on the name, which it bears to this day, "Good Samaritan Children's Home and Rehabilitation Centre."

Chapter 9
HOW MANY LEGS DOES A SPIDER HAVE?

In late 1992, using her considerable powers of persuasion, Mama Mercy was able to convince several local schools to accept some of her charges. Attending elementary school in Kenya required payment of fees for three terms each year, as well as the purchase of a crisp uniform, including shoes. However minor an outlay it might have been—perhaps as little as 5,000 shillings ($50) per year—this could be quite challenging for impoverished parents. Just as American parents struggle to cover college expenses, many Kenyan parents already begin their financial struggle when their children are in elementary school.

Mercy was able to arrange payment plans from the area's schools and was allowed to purchase more affordable secondhand clothing that approximated the official uniforms. She also arranged for the finest elementary school in the area, Huruma Primary, to take two of her children, provided they could pass the entrance interviews. Mercy chose a dozen of her most promising youngsters, including John and Daniel, to compete for the slots. At age nine, John was presented with a marvelous opportunity. Since spending half a year in kindergarten, he had not been in school for nearly five years. Although he had recently received some informal instruction from well-meaning neighbors, he now had a chance to resume his formal education.

The Huruma Primary School sat on eight spacious acres. The campus was comprised of three rectangular two-story buildings, each holding eight classrooms, the administration hall, and a toilet block. In the early '90s, Huruma was situated alongside a fine neighborhood of four-story apartment buildings housing mid-ranking government functionaries. Not long after, however, the housing complex was swallowed by the sprawling Mathare slum, and the apartments slowly deteriorated into shabby tenements.

John sat his interview in a sparsely appointed room in the administration building. He was not so much nervous as simply perplexed at the seemingly random scatter of questions thrown at him by the teachers:

- Fill in the blank to spell an English word—B _ Y
- What number + 1 = 3?
- How many legs does a spider have? A hen? An octopus? A hare?

John and another boy, Musioka Mutungi, performed well and were admitted, John directly into Class Three (third grade) and

Musioka into Class Four. Daniel did not pass muster at Huruma but was enrolled in another local school, Tom Mboya Primary in the adjacent Dandora district, best known as the location of the main garbage dump for Nairobi.

John was a good student with innate curiosity about the world. Over the course of one's primary education, a pupil was expected to take 12 subjects. English and Swahili (Kenya's two national languages) were compulsory, and John liked them best. He also excelled at science and agriculture but struggled with math.

John's classroom at Huruma Primary School

Primary school was a difficult time for John, not that it was academically challenging; rather, the strains of life in the orphanage cast a pall over those years. However generous Mama Mercy, the community, and the donors were, the needs of the orphan children were overwhelming and never ending. John carried two indelible memories of those years—fighting back the ceaseless hunger pangs and, the most bitter, missing his mother.

From Class Three through Class Seven (1993 to 1997), John faced the grim daily choice between eating or going to school. A daily supper of black beans was the sole meal the Good Samaritan orphans could count on. This was all that donor funding could afford. On special occasions an accompaniment of rice or ugali would be added. Because there was no money for firewood however, before supper, each child was required to collect combustibles from the neighborhood in order to earn a full portion of food. This meant that everyone had to scurry home from school, grab a sack, and comb the streets. Because there were few trees in Mathare and Eastleigh, the children would scavenge for scrap wood haphazardly strewn about. Finding the charred fragments of a recently burned dwelling was a bonanza. The trick, though, was to get there before others with the same need for fuel had sacked the site.

The children of Good Samaritan would not go to sleep hungry, but morning was a different matter. According to Mercy's rules, they would awaken daily at five thirty and get ready for school. A thin porridge gruel of maize flour with a pinch of sugar was an infrequent breakfast. Rarely was there water to bathe. John would set off from Good Samaritan on foot in order to arrive by eight o'clock at Huruma Primary, two miles away.

On his way to school, John would often steal food, grabbing a mandazi from a hotel display. Crates of bread stacked in front of a grocery store were another easy target. A friend would boost John up to the top crate, which he'd break open to steal a loaf. Sometimes he'd get caught and slapped by the proprietor, but before the thrashing, John was sure the bread found its way safely into his stomach.

Like many primary schools in Kenya, lunch was not served at Huruma. Children would go home for their midday meal, but for John, this was not possible, since lunch was never served at Good Samaritan. John usually slept through the lunch hour, filling his stomach as best he could with glasses of water. His friends would sometimes bring him a banana or a slice of bread. He always struggled through afternoon classes, worn down and dizzy from hunger.

A typical school day would end at four o'clock, after which several teachers would conduct "preps" for one to two hours. Preps were extra class sessions, which became increasingly important as a student approached graduation and the national secondary school entrance exams. Every day, John faced the decision whether to stay for the supplementary sessions or race back to gather firewood to get his one square meal for the day. Since his personal rule was "stomach first," he usually chose to forego the extra study.

Although he was a bright boy and performed well in school, John frequently skipped class. When he was particularly hungry, he would hide his belongings in a toilet stall. Next, he'd find the prefect (student monitor) for his classroom and threaten him with a beating if he registered John absent. Then John would sneak through the perimeter shrubs, making his way to a busy nearby roundabout. There he would beg for a few shillings to purchase a fried bread biscuit.

On the way home from school, John would find his classmates, and in exchange for cigarettes, he'd finagle the day's lessons for the classes he missed. That night, by candlelight in Good Samaritan, he would make up the exercises. When Mama Mercy would periodically check the children's schoolwork, she would generally find John fully up to date.

John almost got away with his protracted truancy until the day Musioka Mutungi brought home a flyer announcing parents' day at school. John did not have a flyer, and Mama Mercy wanted to know why. He tried to beg out, claiming he didn't get one, but Mercy was no fool. Eventually, she found out that John had been absent when the flyers were passed out. She was perturbed.

At parents' day, the headmaster took Mercy aside and showed her the daily register, which revealed that John had missed almost the entire term. Now she was furious. The next day, she hauled John to school, where he was roundly excoriated and whipped three times by each teacher of the Class Six staff.

* * *

Of the many volunteers who came to assist the children at Good Samaritan, John's favorite was Mrs. Helen. Beginning in 1996 when John was in Class Six, she invited an actor friend, Mr. Kidero, to help her teach acting skills and traditional dance at the orphanage. An ensemble of ten children, six girls and four boys, learned to play a variety of traditional songs from many of Kenya's tribes. The girls sang and danced, while the boys formed the percussion section. John kept time on a cowhide drum, while the others provided accents with gourds and cymbals. After rigorous practice sessions, the children performed throughout Nairobi at community centers and street fairs. Mr. Kidero, who worked at the British Council, the United Kingdom's overseas cultural promotion agency, had extensive connections throughout the city's media circles and arranged to have Kenya Broadcasting Company film drama classes in the now well-known Good Samaritan orphanage. With his natural dramatic flair, John was enraptured with stage performances. This was noticed by Mrs. Helen and Mr. Kidero.

In 1997, Good Samaritan was invited to take part in a nationwide program sponsored by the British Council. The council offered 132 disadvantaged youth throughout Kenya the opportunity to participate in workshops in public speaking. John and Dominique Malonzo, both in Class Seven, were selected to represent Good Samaritan. In addition to lessons on presentation skills, the participants were also taught personal presence, poise, and articulation. The council chose young leaders, who they hoped would return to their homes and instruct others. After several sessions, each participant was expected to give a short speech to the entire assembly. John spoke about life on the streets, a talk that resonated with the audience, many of whom had come from those conditions.

The final session was held at a fancy club in Nairobi, where participants were feted at a luncheon banquet and invited to swim in an Olympic-sized pool. The whole day, John had his eye on a young lady who he decided he was going to try to impress. Not knowing her name, he approached her and asked if she'd like to swim with him.

She immediately caught on to John's game. Without a word, she turned, walked confidently to the diving board, and executed an elegant headfirst dive. On surfacing, she tossed her hair and then looked back to see what John had to offer.

John was flummoxed by her unexpected grace. Now he had to

face the problem that he had never been on a diving board; nor, for that matter, did he know how to swim. But his pride was at stake.

John proceeded to mount the board, walking hesitantly to the end. As it bowed under his weight, he checked his balance, arms waving fitfully. Regaining his composure, he bounced once, awkwardly ... a second time, higher ... and then suddenly, he slipped off the end of the board, narrowly missing his head. A riot of flailing limbs announced his ungainly arrival into the pool.

Dominique Malonzo, watching the entire romantic saga unfold, burst into laughter. After a few hearty guffaws, though, he realized that John had not surfaced. He looked into the deep end and saw John motionless at the bottom of the pool. Of course, John didn't know how to swim! Immediately, Malonzo ran for the lifeguard, who urgently fetched John with calm alacrity onto dry land. The next thing John remembered was water flowing from his mouth as the muscular guard pumped his chest.

The young lady was not impressed.

* * *

Perhaps she might have been impressed though, if he had had the chance to proudly display his plumage at a stage performance rather than take that ill-advised, untested leap into the pool. Alas that opportunity did not present itself until the next year.

Through diligent practice and innate talent, in 1998 while in Class Eight, John earned a colead with Dominique Malonzo in the play *The Queen Mother*. The basic plot was that the queen of a fictitious realm declared that no family could have more than two children. Betrayed by neighbors, a family was turned over to the authorities for having four. John's role was a lawyer defending the family and challenging the law. He worked for three months to prepare his part, memorizing his lines for the ninety-minute production from a forty-eight-page stage play.

To the surprise of the Nairobi community, the Good Samaritan cast won the local competition held on the main stage of the auditorium at the University of Nairobi. That allowed them to proceed to national finals at Tom Mboya Labor College in Kisumu, the largest city in Kenya's western region.

This was the first time John had ever been far outside Nairobi. The festival provided a bus to transport up to thirty-five people. The five actors, plus Mama Mercy and the drama coaches, were accompanied by twenty-five other members of Good Samaritan, who served as cheerleaders.

Before departing, however, Mama Mercy insisted that weekly chores be performed. So, the children awoke at 3:00 a.m. to complete their appointed tasks. Making their way to the National Theatre on the campus of the university, they departed at 8:00 a.m. Singing songs along the way, the exhausted children and spent adults arrived at 11:00 p.m. in Kisumu.

They were boarded at the School for the Deaf—well-appointed accommodations the likes of which they had never seen. Each child had his own mattress and blanket and pillow. In addition, there was a room with a television, ample chairs, and rugs to lie on. The troop spent ten days in Kisumu, after which no one wanted to go home.

At the competition, John and his fellow actors performed brilliantly, taking third place in the nation. This entitled them to advance to the all-African finals in Tunisia. However, this required that everyone have a passport. Since none of the orphans had readily available birth certificates, let alone passports, and Mama Mercy lacked funding, they had neither the time nor the money to arrange the documentation to get to Tunisia. Returning to Nairobi and their daily routine, *The Queen Mother* ended as a bittersweet triumph for the children of Good Samaritan.

* * *

Back at the orphanage, John reverted to some of his unruly habits. In Class Eight, he audaciously skipped virtually an entire three-month term. During this time, he hung out with Gitari and the band in Eastleigh. One night, they had had too much to drink and went back to the base on Galole Street to crash for the night. To cap off the binge, they propped up their heads on stones, telling stories and jokes as they took deep draws from their glue bottles. They noticed that Steven Kivindu wasn't responding to the humorous tales and figured he had passed out.

In the morning, as they were gathering their boxes and sacks, they called to Steven. But again, no response came. They shook him forcefully and then noticed he was as stiff as a statue. He was dead. Without moving his body, John ran to the nearby Pangani Police Station. The officers arrived and performed a cursory inspection. Because Steven had not propped up his head, the glue had run down his throat, dried, and suffocated him. As his body was carried away, the boys saw Steven's glue flask adhered to his lower lip.

John and the others were devastated. They had lost their beloved brother, their roaring protector. John felt an icy loneliness. For days, his soul was an eerie hollow.

Gitari was able to locate Steven's sister, who saw that he was buried in his hometown. Because they had no money, none of the group could attend the funeral. Emotionally drained, John made his way back to Good Samaritan and school.

* * *

Despite his many mischievous dodges, John managed to balance the competing claims of school and hunger. Finally, one teacher stepped forward to challenge him. Mrs. Mwangangi, his history and Christian religious education (CRE) instructor, had recognized both his native intelligence and self-sabotaging delinquency. She became particularly concerned when she observed that John was not taking lunch. She pulled him aside, and he explained the feeding routine at Good Samaritan. Unfamiliar with the orphanage, Mrs. Mwangangi took it upon herself to visit John's home. There, she saw Mercy's bare-bones operation and the heartbreaking circumstances that brought children to Good Samaritan. Some, like John, had been abandoned by their parents. There were those, like Musioka Mutungi, who were sent to Good Samaritan by financially unstable parents. Although they struggled to find 800 shillings ($8) for monthly rent for a single room, they could at least periodically give their son a few shillings for food each day. John did not even have this minimal support.

In 1998, when John reached Class Eight, Mrs. Mwangangi approached the principal, explaining why John could not stay for the after-hours sessions and had missed so much school in prior years. The principal took pity on John and arranged for several teachers to see that he ate from the faculty lunch buffet each day. John was the only pupil at Huruma who enjoyed this special privilege. In addition, he was given a few shillings for daily bus fare.

Sometimes, John took the bus to school, especially during the rainy season, but usually he walked, using the money to buy biscuits for breakfast. However meager the stipend, it meant that John only had to beg on weekends to buy food.

Besides lacking lunch, John also stood out because Mercy could not afford the proper school uniform. Instead of the smart gray shorts that everyone wore, John could always be identified in his scruffy dark blues. For many years, he wore the same short pants until he reached Class Eight, when several teachers noticed that his butt cheeks were showing. When Mrs. Mwangangi was informed, she decided to call a special assembly of the teachers and students to address the problem. Standing with Mrs. Mwangangi in front of 105 students of Class Eight and a dozen teachers, John was deeply embarrassed. Mrs. Mwangangi implored everyone to bring fifteen shillings so they could collectively purchase proper attire for John.

Unaware that Mrs. Mwangangi was going to make a public appeal, John withered with shame. He felt awful to be so poor, degraded to be the only one living in an orphanage, and useless to have to be helped. He started to cry and ran to a seat. About a week later, with the funds collected, John received his new uniform. He was happy finally to be clothed like everyone else, but it was a joy laced with pain that none of the others had probably ever felt.

Beyond the physical straits of relentless hunger, John recalls the pervasive psychological cloud that loomed over the orphanage. So many wished for their parents. How many times did he hear from the children, "I wish I had … I wish I had … I wish I had …"

When John would come home late to the orphanage and had

to forego his dinner, he would also miss his mother. If she had been there, he would have cried, and he knew she would have given him food. But he chose to swallow the pain. He just couldn't dwell on the past. He chose to think about the future, about what he wanted to be.

* * *

As Class Eight came to conclusion, it was time to take the KCPE exams, Kenya Certificate of Primary Education. These national exams not only sealed a student's graduation from elementary school but also served as qualification for the next level of education. Today, Kenya can boast that a relatively high percentage of children finish primary education; fully 80 percent graduate, a significant proportion for a developing country. Unfortunately, there is a pronounced decline in the percentage of the population that goes on to attend high school, only about 25 to 30 percent.[4] This is typically due to the lack of financial support for this more expensive level of education, combined with the pressing need for many to enter the workforce to start earning money. By the time John approached graduation, however, Mama Mercy had lined up sponsors to fund school fees for promising students to continue to secondary school.

In preparing for the exams, John faced a peculiar complication. Registration for the KCPE must be done using three names, one of which was the surname of a parent. For years, John had gone by his baptismal name—his Christian first name, followed by a name honoring a relative. John wasn't exactly sure where the handle "Maina" originated; he believed it was from an elder relative,

[4] Educational Policy Data Center (epdc.orgKenya_coreusaid.pdf).

possibly one of his grandfathers. But he couldn't produce evidence of the surnames of either parent, since neither was to be found. If either had been available, he could have registered as "John Maina Irungu" or "John Maina Wanjiru." So, Mama Mercy came up with a clever solution. John borrowed from her husband's name, James Mwangi Thuo, to create John's official legal name, which he bears to this day—John Maina Thuo.

There were fifteen children from Good Samaritan who sat the exams, including John and Victoria Wanjiko. Shortly before the tests were administered, John missed quite a few days of school. One day, Mercy sent some boys to look for him; they found John hunched over a bottle of glue. When they brought him back to Good Samaritan, Mercy gave him a stern lecture. She baldly stated that, although fifteen pupils from the home would sit the exams, there were funds for only fourteen to attend secondary school. Furthermore, she was confident that thirteen would perform adequately to qualify. However, she was not so sure about him and Victoria. Because of his persistent truancy and glue sniffing, Mercy told him that he and Victoria were competing for last place.

John sat the exams, and as soon as they were finished, he was back on the streets, not seen around Good Samaritan for weeks. Exam results for all students in Kenya were publicly posted at the same time throughout the nation, usually about one month after the conclusion of testing. When results were announced, John went to Good Samaritan and asked Mama Mercy how he had done. Since results were disclosed through a unique code for each student, Mercy, quite annoyed to see him, said she didn't know, and he should get them himself.

Through stealthy enquiry, John had learned that Victoria's score was 295 "marks" (points) out of a possible 700, a respectable, though hardly outstanding, score. With this information, John made his way over to Huruma Primary and into the administration building. Posted on a large bulletin board were the results for every student in the school. John ran his finger down the dense column of numbers, landing on his code, 033, next to which were his marks—307. John was going to secondary school!

He was so excited that he dashed out of the building and up to the Juja Road. He leapt on the tailgate of the first passing truck, his glue bottle proudly raised as he cheered aloud all the way to the abandoned Esso station. He jumped off the moving truck and ran down the hill to Good Samaritan. Hiding his glue bottle, he burst into Mama Mercy's office and gave her the news.

She grimaced.

One month later, his tuition funds arrived.

Chapter 10
GOOD PLANS

In January 1999, shortly after turning fifteen, John Maina entered Form One (freshman year) at the Maina Wanjigi Secondary School. Maina Wanjigi was in Eastleigh on 4th Street adjacent to the Moi Air Force Base, within a few blocks of the garbage dump where John used to sell materials and not far from the Shamshudin Hotel. In Kenya, there is a distinction between a "secondary school" and a "high school." Students like John receiving marks of 300 to 450 on their KCPE exams were admitted to secondary school, and the best students, garnering marks above 450, attended high schools. Although not one of the top schools in Nairobi, Maina Wanjigi was an up-and-coming institution. As important as attending school was the friendship John would develop with Mrs. Maina, a loving teacher who became his mentor.

Why so many Mainas—Maina Wanjigi, Mrs. Maina, John Maina?

The nation of Kenya was formed by harnessing together forty-two African tribes within boundaries established by European powers at the Congress of Berlin in 1884/85. The late nineteenth century marked the "Scramble for Africa," as England, France, Germany, Belgium, Portugal, and the Netherlands occupied and dominated the last great unconquered continent on earth. The British were granted rights to the Kenyan territory, among other vast tracts in east and south Africa. In order to rule Kenya effectively, they allied themselves with the dominant tribe in the region, the Kikuyus. Still to this day, the Kikuyus are Kenya's largest tribe, comprising between 20 and 25 percent of the country's population. They are also the politically and commercially ascendant tribe in the nation.

Tribes are comprised of many clans and subclans, and the Maina clan is one of the largest among Kikuyus; hence, its name is one of the most common. But just as many Irish Americans bear the Kennedy surname, not all Kennedys are wealthy. In the same way, not all Mainas are well-to-do. The Honorable James Maina Wanjigi was a wealthy, powerful cabinet secretary, entrepreneur, and philanthropist who founded a secondary school. Then there are other Mainas—Mrs. Maina, a schoolteacher, and John Maina, an abandoned orphan.

John enjoyed secondary school much more than elementary school, mostly because lunch was provided every day. With that basic need fulfilled, school allowed him the opportunity to acquire an education to pursue his dreams with more energy and stamina. In secondary school, students followed twelve subjects. English, Swahili, and math were compulsory throughout Kenya. Some schools, such as Maina Wanjigi, also required biology and chemistry. John was a good, though not outstanding student. He did well in English, African history, and CRE. These performances were offset by weak ones in biology, chemistry, and especially math, which he barely passed.

Like students the world over, John's daily routine was regimented by the school schedule:

5:00	Wake at Good Samaritan, bathe, take tea, walk half a mile to school
7:30	Arrive at school
8:00–10:15	Early-morning classes *(three modules of forty-five minutes)*
10:15–10:30	Break
10:30–12:45	Three late-morning classes
12:45–1:45	Lunch
1:45–4:00	Three afternoon classes

After four o'clock, some of the students remained for interscholastic sport practice and competition. During John's time, there were only two sports—football (soccer) and athletics (track and field). John was a goalie and striker on the football team. He was respectably good and played on teams that advanced well through the national secondary school tournament bracket. Unsurprisingly, his aggressive street behavior carried over to the football pitch.

One afternoon, John's team from Maina Wanjigi was playing the neighboring boys' squad from Pumwani Secondary School. John was in goal, and his team was ahead by a score of 3–2 well into the second half. At the seventy-five-minute mark, about fifteen minutes before the end of the game, the lead striker from Pumwani broke through Maina Wanjigi's last two defenders and was bearing down on John. The striker took a ferocious shot; John made a leaping dive and caught the ball. With adrenalin coursing through his veins, overcome by the thrill of the moment, John triumphantly flipped off the striker. Justifiably offended, the striker got in John's face, at which point John threw a punch. Chaos ensued as both benches emptied onto the field in a melee of fisticuffs and curses. When the referees were finally able to establish order, they sensibly called off the game, won 3–2 by Maina Wanjigi, thanks to John's fantastic save and provocative antics.

* * *

In the meantime, Mama Mercy was busy with expansion plans for Good Samaritan. Over the course of about six months, from late 1997 through early 1998, a huge flood caused by the El Niño effect altered the course of the Mathare River. It no longer swung a loop close to the road with the steep bank directly opposite Good Samaritan; rather the flood straightened the flow such that fifty yards of dry land now appeared between the cliff and the new riverbed.

As Good Samaritan was growing in number, and with unoccupied plots scarce in Mathare, Mama Mercy adopted an aggressive approach to land acquisition. In 1999, after the newly opened land between the cliff and the riverbed stabilized, Mercy hired a tractor to reshape the terrain. She had the near vertical fall turned into a sloping pitch, still quite steep but able to support small buildings. Then she quickly erected sheds for cows and pigs on the slope, allowing them to graze on the flatter ground near the river.

What right did she have to grab land, alter the contour of the terrain, and set up the only grazing pasture in congested Mathare? None, of course. But once again, where property rights and title deeds are dubious, Mama Mercy aggressively exercised the time-honored rights of a squatter. Besides, if she were ever challenged, she would simply plead that the land used to graze animals was strictly for the benefit of the dozens of orphans in her care. She reckoned that no authority would dare challenge her—and no one ever has.

In 2000, an anonymous private party made a large contribution to significantly expand the facilities of Good Samaritan, which took five months to complete. Engineering and architecture students from Kenyatta University laid out the plans, and interns from Kenya Polytechnic installed the wiring and plumbing. A ten-foot wall was erected along the perimeter enclosing the compound. A double panel iron gate, which secured street access, was painted bright blue, lending an inviting cheerfulness amid the slum's drab matte grays and browns. The enclosed space delineated a yard of hard-packed dirt on which the children could play, protected from Mathare's seamy elements. Toilet and shower facilities with sturdy cement floors were placed on the plot just inside the main entrance gate. The entire area behind Mama Mercy and Thuo's apartment, which had housed boys, girls, a small classroom, and the chicken coop, was converted into the boys' dormitory. Erected above the apartment was a two-story wooden structure. The ground floor housed the main office and a storeroom. Stairs to the second floor led to the girls' dorm and four small classrooms. John was overjoyed with the new structure. The rooms were larger, affording more space for sleeping and studying. For the first time, the compound enjoyed electricity, which meant the children could now study at ease, not crowded around the few candles that Mama Mercy could afford.

* * *

Throughout school, John never lost his street boy penchant for mischief. During secondary school, he developed a taste for alcohol. Breakfast at Good Samaritan continued to be an erratic offering. Porridge was the customary serving, but that was nothing more than boiled water and flour, enhanced by a pinch of sugar and an occasional thin dollop of Blue Band margarine. When breakfast was served, it was often too late for John to consume before having to head off to school. To energize himself in the morning, he would swing by a changa'a den run by a friend of his mother. There he'd wait until an acquaintance would order a glass of the illegal alcohol and let John take a swig. He'd then continue to Maina Wanjigi.

He'd also fortify himself at the morning school break. John and a few buddies would sneak off campus through a hidden path behind the dining hall. They called it the *panya* route, the "rat track." Once safely off school premises, the boys would gulp booze, smoke a joint, or take a few hits of glue. And who was often there to enjoy the break? Gitari, of course, usually offering him a shot of changa'a. To mask their caper, John and his classmates would pop some menthol sweets in their mouths and sneak back into the schoolyard in time to join the second set of classroom modules. Now mellow, he felt he always returned from break "feeling like a gentleman." After drinking his morning meals, John's first solid food was lunch served at school. He'd round out the day with the standard serving of beans for dinner at Good Samaritan. A touch of changa'a as a nightcap would help him fall asleep.

By Form Two (sophomore year), John was a strapping young man, and his girlfriend, Margaret, now in Class Eight, had matured into a young woman. Puppy love was no longer enough for them. Adjacent to the orphanage was a set of rental rooms erected by Mama Mercy and Thuo when they initially built on the property. Over the years, John had ingratiated himself to Mr. Mongote, one of the long-standing residents, by occasionally supplying him with food spirited from Good Samaritan's kitchen. When the young couple desired some intimate privacy, John called in favors, arranging for Mr. Mongote to slip him the keys to his room and disappear for a few hours.

* * *

John was exposed to Christianity as a young child. His mother and Njeri would walk the children to church every Sunday. Mama Mercy, a woman of deep faith, would pray frequently in the shelter and saw that the children regularly attended Sunday worship services.

Kenya does not espouse the separation of church and state as in the United States and other Western countries. With over 80 percent of its citizens devout, practicing Christians, state schools such as Huruma Primary offer Christian religious education as part of their basic curriculum at all class levels. At Maina Wanjigi, John rigorously delved into religion, principally because of the encouragement he received from Mrs. Maina, his biology and chemistry teacher for the entire four years. Sharing a common surname, Mrs. Maina took to John from the outset. She was also familiar with Good Samaritan, having previously visited the orphanage, and was aware of John's hardscrabble life journey.

Mrs. Maina kept an eye on John and saw that he would sometimes come late to school looking bedraggled. Most teachers would routinely punish latecomers. However, Mrs. Maina had sympathy for John's circumstances. She'd ask why he looked so dejected. When he explained that there had been no breakfast at Good Samaritan that day, she would often give him twenty shillings and allow him to leave the school compound to take tea.

Grateful for Mrs. Maina's understanding and generosity, John devised his own meal plan. Each day when lunch was served, John was sure to be the first one to the cafeteria. He'd always dress neatly, with his shirt tucked in and tie straightened. The buffet attendants thought that this respectable-looking chap certainly deserved to be served immediately. So, John proceeded to marshal a heaping plate before the monitor arrived to punch his meal card. Quickly inhaling his food, John would repair to the recess yard to allow the meal to settle. Just before the end of lunch period, however, John would then reappear at the end of the line. To disguise himself, he'd now appear disheveled, with shirttails flying and his tie at half-mast. This time, he'd dutifully present his meal card and gleefully collect an entire second helping.

His deception worked for a while, until an eagle-eyed chef caught onto the scheme. He reported John to the deputy headmaster, who promptly hauled John into his office. Fortunately, Mrs. Maina was also called in. Familiar with the situation, she defended John and then made a provocative recommendation—since John knew all the lunchroom tricks, he should be the dining hall monitor.

Deferring to Mrs. Maina's wisdom, the deputy headmaster agreed to her suggestion. For the final two years at Maina Wanjigi, John oversaw the lunchroom line.

Mrs. Maina's influence on John's life went far beyond satisfying the incessant hunger pangs of a teenage boy. She encouraged him to join the school's Christian Union (CU), a national, nondenominational student organization whose main purpose was to foster the development of Christian principles among its members. She was the faculty sponsor. In addition, the mission of the Christian Union was to support the underprivileged, especially street boys and orphans. John joined CU in Form One and enjoyed attending the school rallies.

Eventually, he became a CU coordinator, whose chief responsibility was to announce meetings and promote attendance. CU struck a chord with John, inspiring him to want to become a judge or lawyer to help those in need. He had lived that life, personally experiencing the struggles of the poor. He knew how those who lacked money also lacked access to justice. He wanted the less privileged to have a voice. Mrs. Maina counseled him that pursuing a legal career would require strong performance in history, Swahili, and CRE. Fortunately for John, these were all subjects in which he excelled.

As their relationship deepened, Mrs. Maina decided to take John aside to offer personal advice. She'd sit with him in the staff room and ask what he wanted for his future. John had never given it a thought. Nor had anyone ever asked him. She knew that John had been a hellion in primary school and was aware of his extramural shenanigans at the other end of the panya route.

She admonished him to stop smoking and drinking. How many parents have made those speeches and how often have they been disregarded? But these had a profound impact on John because of the tremendous respect he held for Mrs. Maina. It wasn't that John changed immediately—he continued to indulge his habits—but Mrs. Maina kept instilling her message, confident that someday he would come around.

In Forms One and Two, John couldn't function without alcohol and glue. Although using them adversely affected his concentration in class, he'd feel dizzy and break out in cold sweats without these crutches. Slowly he reduced his drinking. By 2001 in Form Three, he stopped going down the panya route. In 2002, in Form Four, Mrs. Maina showed him a thirty-second video clip which graphically depicted the debilitating long-term effects of glue on the lungs and brain. John has not sniffed glue since then.

As they became closer, Mrs. Maina confided in John her own life's challenges. Her husband was a drunkard, beginning his day with three beers and ending with many more. She prayed he would eventually stop, and she needed encouragement to see her way through her travails. She told him that she understood the difficulty of living in a children's home but that this would be temporary. She shared with him two of her favorite Bible verses, which she encouraged him to recite every morning upon waking, especially when things weren't going well. He first heard them when he was in Form Two and has recited them every day since then. "Surely goodness and mercy shall follow me all the days of my life: and I will dwell in the house of the Lord forever" (Psalm 23:6 KJV). And his favorite from the book of Jeremiah (29:11 NIV): "'For I know the plans I have for you,' declares the Lord, 'plans to prosper...and not to harm you, plans to give you hope and a future.'"

John loved Mrs. Maina, not because of the subjects she taught him but because of the time she spent with him and the encouragement she gave him. No one had ever given him hope for a bright future. He memorized the two Bible verses to which he clung throughout his life, always believing that, no matter what he was going through, deep inside, he knew that God had good plans for him.

Chapter 11
WOODEN SLATS

From the time John and Daniel moved into Mama Mercy's quarters in 1991, they had spotted their mother every week or two wandering the streets. She was always disoriented, probably drunk, in the evenings usually coming from the direction of a bar. Afraid and bewildered, they always kept their distance, observing warily from afar.

Keziah knew her children were living in Good Samaritan. When she passed the orphanage, she'd frequently pretend to fall and remain lying on the ground. This embarrassed her children, since there were some orphans at the home who knew their story and recognized their mother lying prostrate outside the gate. On one occasion when she collapsed in front of Good Samaritan, Daniel went out and slapped her back to consciousness. When she awoke, she stumbled to her feet and ran along the street and up the hill.

In 2001, a friend came to Good Samaritan and told John that his mother was dead. She had been found on 6th Street, one of the dark lanes in Eastleigh. She had probably been hit by a vehicle as she stumbled drunkenly through the night, left on the side of the road to die. The news came on December 14, just two days after his eighteenth birthday. John was at once shocked and relieved; his mother's long nightmare was finally over. His friend told him that her body was being held at Kenyatta National Hospital. One of John's friends worked at the mortuary and offered to help get the body released without having to pay fees.

As the eldest son, Daniel took the lead in making arrangements for the funeral. Dutifully, he spoke with the two aunts, Keziah's sisters, who had not made the slightest effort to help her children through more than a decade of struggle. As expected, the two were obstreperous, insisting that she did not deserve to be buried in the family plot in Murang'a. They claimed she had not attended their father's funeral years ago. So rather than disgrace the family grounds, the aunts wanted her to be interred in the dilapidated Langata Cemetery, where the poorest, most dispossessed were laid to rest. Unwilling to accept this mortal insult to the memory of their mother, Daniel took the trip to Murang'a to speak with his grandmother, Keziah's mother. Not harboring the same grudges or ill-will as her other daughters, the grandmother wanted Keziah close by, next to her father on the family grounds.

Daniel returned and told John and Jane the good news that their mother would receive a respectable burial. John and Daniel got to work, creating a makeshift coffin from wooden slats that had been used as concrete forms for the construction of the new toilet block at Good Samaritan. One of John's friends, a budding artist, painted her name and dates on the coffin lid— "Keziah Wanjiru, 1958–2001."

They took the homemade box to the mortuary in which her body was placed. Friends contributed funds to rent a pickup truck to transport her coffin and the children fifty miles to the family home in Murang'a. As his uncle drove the truck along the highway, John had many flashbacks to life with his mother, especially about the love and concern she'd always showed him. For so many years, he had hoped she would be cured of whatever was plaguing her. He'd wanted to be reunited as a family. He had so many questions he wanted to ask her: Who was Daniel's father? Why did you and James Irungu separate? Why did you drink so much?

He looked down at the makeshift coffin and could not believe that his dearest mother would be buried in such a shabby, makeshift crate. He had dreamed that one day he would be a rich, successful lawyer and buy her a home. Now he just felt lonely, missing the tender presence of his mother.

Turning off the highway, the vehicle slowed in the congestion. Over three tortuous miles, they eventually reached their destination. Along the way, pedestrians gazed into the truck bed to view the load. This most private moment with his mother was being desecrated by idle curiosity seekers. In the heat of the day, the corpse began to emit an odor detectable by all. John was ashamed. Humiliated, he opened the lid and took a last glance at his mother as he sprayed a perfume over her remains.

On December 28, 2001, Keziah Wanjiru was buried in the backyard of the family homestead next to her father's grave. John thanked his grandmother for allowing her to be buried at home. No certificate records her death or its cause.

Chapter 12
DOWN SOUTH

In November 2002, one month before his nineteenth birthday, John took the battery of national secondary school leaving exams. Good marks would allow him a place at a technical college, and top scores would earn a seat at a university. Twelve from Good Samaritan were sitting the exams—John from Maina Wanjigi, seven girls from St. Theresa's, and four boys from the Eastleigh school.

John had just finished the final test in science, and he and the others met up and were making their way back to Good Samaritan. Everyone was jubilant. The celebration began by undoing their formal school attire. Shirts were unbuttoned, tails untucked, and ties loosened. They had made it through secondary school!

At five o'clock, they arrived to see Mama Mercy standing outside the gate looking angry. They thought she might be waiting to punish an errant child. She remained stiff and silent until everyone had arrived, her gaze focused in the distance. Without explanation, she ordered all of them out of the home immediately. "None of you are going to enter through this gate," she growled.

Everyone was stunned. What was going on? At first, they thought she was joking as she was known to do; surely this was a just a prank she was pulling on the joyous students. Besides, Mama Mercy had never given any warning that she was going to evict them. Her scowl deepened as she shouted, "If you don't believe me, look down south where your boxes are." She pointed to their metal boxes, which had been removed from the orphanage dormitories and rolled down the steep hill that ended at the river— "down south" as it was known in Good Samaritan.

Now it was clear that she was not joking. Some asked desperately, "Mama, what's going on? Where do you want us to go?"

Seeing the incident unfold, neighbors intervened and asked why the youngsters were being so unceremoniously chased away. What were they supposed to do? Why hadn't they at least been given some notice?

Pressed from all sides, Mercy finally offered an explanation. She had just learned that the law did not allow minors over eighteen years old to reside in orphanages. She was concerned that, if the municipal children's officer visited the home, she would be fined, and he would demand that everyone over eighteen be immediately dismissed from the premises. Clearly concerned, Mercy had to make a dramatic statement lest the authorities discover her lapse, so she'd ordered boys from the orphanage to roll the metal boxes down the hill. This also served as a harsh warning to next year's graduates to plan ahead.

Angry and distressed, Mercy turned around, walked into the compound, and slammed the gate. The despondent students trudged down the hill to fetch their belongings. Boxes without padlocks had opened, and their contents were strewn along the hillside. John was fortunate that his box was locked. He opened it and saw that all his worldly possessions were in order—four trousers (two for his school uniform and two for casual wear), two shirts, two pairs of shoes, socks, and undergarments.

Most of the children said that they planned to go to an aunt or uncle living in the city, but John had no one. His parents were gone; his brother was living with friends who had no more space; and even though his aunts lived only two minutes away, he wanted nothing to do with them. He sat on his box, composing himself, tempering his anger, and reflecting on what to do. He knew that he needed to go where his friends were, where he'd be accepted. So, he carried his box up the hill to a changa'a den about two blocks from Good Samaritan.

Thus began the darkest, most desultory period of John's life.

PART III
SURVIVAL
—————— 2003-2008 ——————

When it is dark enough,
you can see the stars.

—Ralph Waldo Emerson

Chapter 13
KIUMANE: DORIS DAY'S GOT STREET CRED

All that John dreamt of had been ruined. He couldn't see any future before him. He had been a student for the past ten years and had dealt with the challenges of growing up in an orphanage. He figured that, in three or four years, he'd arrive at a good place in life; maybe he'd even be prospering. But now what was he going to do? Instead of being able to go on to higher education, John was forced out of his home for the second time in his life.

About two blocks from Good Samaritan was a changa'a den run by an enterprising woman who had opened six bars in some of the toughest slums in Nairobi—Mathare, Eastleigh, and the neighboring slums of Dandora and Kayoli. Her name was Wangu, which in her native Kikuyu tongue means "the ruthless one." And that she had to be in her line of business. She had been a good friend of John's mother and had spent many afternoons in their apartment talking for hours with Keziah.

The Gathare Bar in which Keziah had worked served an upscale working-class clientele, trade professionals with steady occupations—masons, plumbers, electricians. Gathare served branded products, especially Tusker, Kenya's internationally famous premium beer.

Wangu's dens, on the other hand, catered to casual laborers working on the fringes of the economy—maize roasters, cart pullers, and construction site day laborers, beasts of burden hauling cinder block and rebar up many flights of scaffolding. These workers' wages were so erratic that they could not reliably earn enough to keep a rented room. Their preferred drink was the crystal clear changa'a from riverside distilleries. A glass went for twenty shillings, less than one-third the price of a Tusker, and was several times more potent, cost-effectively delivering the desired effect.

Wangu named this den Kiumane, which had the same meaning (with less saccharine lilt) as the title of Doris Day's 1960s hit, "Que Sera, Sera (Whatever Will Be, Will Be)". And the next line of the song was also apt, though far more ominous, for the patrons of the establishment who routinely drank themselves into oblivion— "The future's not ours to see. Que sera, sera."

Changa'a dens were humble bare-bones establishments, whose purpose was to provide potent drink and neighborly camaraderie for patrons to get thoroughly smashed. A den was nothing more than a low structure, more or less twenty-foot-by-twenty-foot, fashioned of scrap materials—wood, plastic, and metal sheeting. Ill-fitting boards allowed light to filter through during the day; one light bulb hung from the ceiling illuminating the room at night.

The Kiumane changa'a den and its clientele

Furniture was simply beaten up, mismatched wooden tables and benches. When fully packed on a Saturday night, a den might accommodate up to twenty-five customers.

Wangu was one of the big shots in the area. She drove a fancy Toyota Corolla station wagon, which she'd load with changa'a canisters. Its heavily tinted windows allowed her to discreetly deliver illicit brew to her various locales.

Most bar owners in the area were women because they were most effective in dealing with the authorities. In order to operate a changa'a den, it was essential to obtain a "license" from the local OCS (officer commanding station), the head of the local constabulary. The license was nothing more than a negotiated agreement for the bar owner to make monthly payments to the OCS and the officer's squad to allow the den to sell its delicious, potent, but highly illegal changa'a. Women were much more adept at sweet talking the OCSs, where men would too often get pushy and quarrelsome. Since the lowest-ranking patrol officers were routinely cycled between stations, the OCS had to instruct each new incoming group which establishments to let alone during their beat patrols.

* * *

John picked up his box from down south, trudged up the steep slope to the street in front of Good Samaritan, and made his way down two blocks to Kiumane. He dropped his box in the corner and went back to help the other outcast students.

Several hours later, Wangu arrived and immediately saw the storage box. At first upset, she was told it belonged to Maina and that he was having problems. At about this time, John arrived and explained to her the sad train of events. Taking pity on him, she embraced John, exclaiming, "You are my son. You can sleep here."

Wangu also needed help at the bar. Dens did not have the same liquor cages as bars like Gathare. Rather, there was a bar master who poured drink from bottles continually filled from the twenty-liter jerricans brought directly from the river distilleries. She was assisted by a few others who helped keep order in small crowded rooms that could quickly become disorderly.

At first, John performed the simple tasks of cleaning the room and hauling water. In exchange for his services, he was allowed to sleep in the den after it closed and keep his metal trunk in the storeroom. John called the Kiumane his home for three years, from the end of 2002 when he was forced out of Good Samaritan, until the end of 2005. Two other assistants were also permitted to put up in the den.

At twenty-two years old, James Mwangi was four years older

than John. His nickname was Mudu Muriu ("Blackie") because of his extremely dark skin. He and his family were from Thika, a small industrial city north of Nairobi. His situation echoed so many others; Mudu Muriu's father had died and his mother had brought the family fifteen miles down the highway into Nairobi. For a while, he'd roamed the streets collecting scrap materials just as John had done as a boy. He'd always been sure to give his mother money from his work on the streets, and he'd always been sure to keep a few shillings for himself to buy changa'a at Kiumane, which he'd frequently pass on his scavenging routes. Eventually, Mudu Muriu became a regular, and Wangu took him in to fill two important roles.

One critical function at all changa'a dens was the lookout who patrolled the area outside the front door. Mudu Muriu's job was to alert Wangu if police were in the near vicinity. If they were approaching the premises, she'd intercept the officers in the street to make sure they were aware that she had a fully paid license. Mudu Muriu also performed the critical task of keeping the den stocked with changa'a. When new supplies were needed, he'd carry a twenty-liter jerrican, weighing nearly fifty pounds, half a mile from the riverside stills.

John Munya-Uki was known a "Kafupi," meaning "Shorty," because of his diminutive height. At thirty-five, he was quite a bit older than the others and boasted a résumé that was as suspect as it was sensational. Kafupi claimed he had been a member of the feared administrative police force during the twenty-four-year dictatorial reign of President Daniel arap Moi (1978–2002). He bragged about the time that he was a member of a security team escorting an armored truck filled with cash on its way to Nairobi. As they proceeded, the squad decided to make off with the loot, turned the vehicle around, and headed for the border. As the tale unfolded, Kafupi and his cohorts were captured crossing into Uganda. He and the others received fifteen-year sentences. Released only a few years ago, Kafupi had become an itinerant cobbler, repairing shoes throughout Nairobi's slums. As an offshoot of his business, he learned to repair holes in the metal basins used by the poor to prepare their food. Wangu employed him once for a repair and realized his value to her operation. She allowed him to sleep in the den every night in exchange for mending all damaged changa'a canisters.

During the week, John, Mudu Muriu, and Kafupi would sleep without a blanket on the bare dirt floor, huddled together for warmth. While the lack of bedding was incommodious, the prevalence of lice bothered John most. On weekends, and especially after paydays, upward of fifteen people would be accommodated in Kiumane. Most of the crowd consisted of those who could not afford a regular shelter but had fulfilled the basic house requirement of purchasing enough changa'a to earn a spot on the floor.

In time, John proved himself an honorable, trustworthy employee and moved up to the role of "prefect" or steward of the den. In this role, he acquired the responsibility to keep track of the den's glasses. Changa'a is served in simple six-ounce clear glasses, like those used to serve breakfast juices. Each morning, John would count the glasses and, at closing, take inventory again to make sure the stock remained constant. During busy drinking hours, he'd be sure to watch that no one pocketed a glass. One of the common tricks was to pilfer a glass, move along to the next den, and exchange the glass for a free drink. The incentive for the prefect to keep close watch on the glasses was that he was personally responsible for any that went missing. The only exception was if a customer accidentally broke a glass. After a long stretch in which no glasses went missing, Wangu would give John a 200-shilling ($2) tip.

The other major responsibility of the prefect was to monitor the den during off hours. When the room shut down, John would padlock the door from the inside, safekeeping the facility and alcohol, and ensuring that the night's guests would be unable to steal product and sneak away. The next day, when the proprietor would announce herself with a brisk knock, John would unlock the door and empty the provisional dormitory.

One morning, a purveyor of changa'a knocked early to make a delivery. John got himself going and told the others it was time to clear out. One very drunken fellow from the previous night couldn't seem to rouse himself. John poked and prodded at Wakiman, but he wasn't responding. This wasn't unusual. Wakiman was a construction worker and daily customer at Kiumane. Every evening, he'd be good for three or four glasses of changa'a and would often need one or two in the morning to get his motor started. Figuring he was horribly hungover, several lads dragged him outside, placing him in the sun, expecting that the warmth and brightness would awaken him. After a couple of hours, John found that Wakiman was not moving but had expired.

Now John, Mudu Muriu, and Kafupi became concerned. Their first reaction was to fear that the police might suspect them of having poisoned Wakiman. After deliberating, though, they decided it best to simply report the death, a rather common occurrence in changa'a dens in the slums. So, one of the assistants called the police, who sent a Land Cruiser to transport the body to the mortuary—no questions asked.

Chapter 14
STILLS, CARTS, AND SEWERS

Although John enjoyed a room at Kiumane, he was not paid in cash. Nor did he receive any food. So, he had to look for other jobs. That took him back to the relatively more prosperous Eastleigh.

For a young man in John's socioeconomic class, finding gainful employment in Kenya was extremely difficult. Youth unemployment and underemployment were difficult to determine, but a reasonable estimate would be collectively around 40 to 50 percent, especially in the slums. Obtaining a job often required a "godfather" who could pull strings. But nothing of the kind was available to John, so he needed to make his way resourcefully on the streets.

Although he was a veteran street boy, living on the streets at the age of twenty was different than doing so as a child of five, six, or seven years old. Children collected scrap materials to earn money; older boys cobbled together a living through a variety of odd jobs.

It was the need to pay for illegal alcohol that propelled John to seek employment. It's said that there are those who live to work and those who work to live. John worked to drink.

John had become an alcoholic in the years after departing Good Samaritan. He'd enjoyed his first sips of alcohol when he was in primary school. On his ventures to the roundabout to beg, he would sometimes use the small cash handouts to try some alcohol. But at that time, this was only a sporadic fancy. The roots of his addiction started in secondary school with friends who escaped daily via the panya route. If he was going to hang out with the group, he had to drink and get drunk—peer pressure is the same the world over.

Stills at the riverside

There was no shortage of opportunities to obtain affordable drink in Mathare, the changa'a capital of Kenya. Along the Mathare River, enterprising groups set up industrial-scale stills and produced the finest hooch in the country. One site might have as many as a dozen stills operating round the clock with a well-rehearsed division of labor assigned to each task of the production process.

Making changa'a begins with fermentation. A twenty-liter canister is filled with a mixture of water, yeast, and a sweetener—either plain white table sugar, natural sugar cane, or molasses. This mixture is allowed to ferment for three days, after which it is ready for distillation.

One group of workers hauls the canisters down to the site. A twenty-liter can weighs nearly fifty pounds, and most workers lug two at a time to the mouth of the still. The still itself is a marvelous contraption, a testament to the brilliance of do-it-yourself engineering. Each still is constructed out of one and a half 55-gallon metal petroleum barrels. The half barrel serves as a firepit set on the ground and is continuously stoked with firewood. The bottom of the full barrel is placed at a forty-five-degree angle atop this furnace base such that it protrudes over the edge of the lower half barrel. From the side, the still looks like an old cannon, with the lower half as the mount and the full drum as the cannon muzzle angling upward.

To begin the process, the distiller spins a lever, which opens the top of the tightly sealed barrel. In goes the fermented mash, and the lever is reversed to reseal the chamber. As the solution boils, an alcohol-rich vapor leaves the chamber through a plastic tube at the top of the barrel. This tube runs down to the river and is connected to a ten-foot coil of fine copper tubing that sits in the water. As the vapor passes through the copper coil, it is cooled by the river water and condenses back to a liquid state. The liquid flows through a final length of plastic tubing to another twenty-liter canister sitting on shore, which captures the fresh elixir. The entire process takes thirty to forty-five minutes and yields some of the finest, most potent clear alcohol in all of Kenya.

When John was low on cash, he would occasionally go down to one of the sites and offer his services. Since he worked in a bar owned by one of the big bosses, all the distillers knew him. In exchange for carrying the heavy canisters from the warehouse, John was given the enviable task of tasting the fresh moonshine. Just like an expert wine taster, John learned to distinguish the finest changa'a, which was odorless, from inferior product, whose sour bouquet and bitter taste hinted at adulterated base mash. Of course, just as a wine aficionado uses bread between samples, John munched a fried mandazi to clarify his palette between tastings.

But this was an infrequent manner of supporting himself. The most common task was serving as a porter, carrying other people's belongings. The best place to offer these services was at the bus stage (bus stop) at the junction of 1st Avenue and 12th Street, the busy confluence of many bus routes. A street boy needed to be discerning about positioning himself at the stage. It made no sense to wait at the stops for the local routes from the Dandora or Mathare slums because these riders probably didn't carry luggage. Besides, they were likely to be poor and unable to offer a tip. The best stops were those from Mandera, Garissa, and Wajir, the large desert cities in northeastern Kenya. These travelers were usually well-to-do Somalis coming to "Little Mogadishu." John did well by the Somalis since they spoke little Swahili but were proficient in English, which John now spoke fluently. They would come with loads of luggage and often bring containers of camel milk, a Somali staple not easily found in Nairobi.

John would carry the bundles either a few blocks to their destination or just a few steps to a waiting taxi. For his services, he would garner tips of fifty to a hundred shillings. His best friend at the time was a strong, muscular lad from the Luo tribe in western Kenya, who called himself "Panya Mlenge," which means "Confused Rat." Just as a rat will frantically dart from place to place, the hardworking Panya Mlenge would feverishly move between Eastleigh and Mathare, carrying heavy sacks of potatoes and cabbages that no one else could handle.

Like so many other street boys, Panya Mlenge had attained only a fifth- or sixth-grade education. He noticed how John stood out from the rest of the boys, since he had completed secondary school. One day, Panya Mlenge took John aside and, from a most sincere corner of his heart, implored him to find a better job. He believed that John belonged to a higher social class and had no business on the streets. As Panya Mlenge spoke, John began to feel upset about the course his life had taken—how adverse circumstances had eclipsed his good intentions. He took Panya Mlenge's plea as words of encouragement; it boosted his morale. He felt that, someday, someone would recognize his talents and that eventually he would rise off the streets.

John spent many days at the bus stage in his early years on the street. He was too small to carry heavy loads, but he could beg. At that time, the most successful technique was to provide unsolicited shoeshines. Before engaging the customers, John knew it was important to hide his glue bottle. Most adults were reluctant to give a handout if they thought it was going to purchase an intoxicating substance. Even though John fully intended the proceeds for that errant purpose, he needed to be discreet. With the glue flask well hidden, he would scout out travelers with dusty shoes. Without asking, he'd bend down and wipe them with a clean cloth, rise with one hand outstretched, and look them directly in the eye. Often, he'd receive a small coin of five, ten, or maybe even twenty shillings. If he started at morning rush hour, he could usually meet his daily target of 200 shillings by evening.

But begging was for boys; hauling was for men. Another common hauling job was operating a handcart. Handcarts are transport vehicles found everywhere in Kenya. A handcart is a simple wooden flatbed mounted on an axle attached to old car or truck tires. A crossbar at the front allows the operator to push and steer. The streets are filled with handcarts, whose drivers serve as the delivery arms for local shops. Carts are also hired out on a daily basis to casual laborers.

John and his friends would sometimes hire a cart and deliver clean water throughout the neighborhood. Renting the cart would cost about fifty shillings per day, and they'd pay two shillings to fill a twenty-liter canister. They'd then deliver a canister to the customer's room for ten shillings. Since water is heavy and many cans had to be delivered to make the outing commercially worthwhile, it was exhausting work.

By far the most lucrative but also the filthiest and most dangerous job was unblocking sewer lines. When modern permanent residential construction began in Mathare in the mid-twentieth century, the municipal government laid basic sewer lines, which routed effluent from multistory apartment buildings directly into the Mathare River (the same river in which lay the copper tubing to cool the changa'a). As residential construction exploded in the valley, private developers set their own sewer lines, with the objective of routing the wastewater from the building into whatever outdoor pipes they could tap. This resulted in a knotty skein of conduits and manholes running just beneath the surface of Mathare's maze of thoroughfares and footpaths.

None of these was well maintained, and many had cracked and leaked or even partially collapsed. All were susceptible to clogging. Careless tenants disposed of cotton balls, avocado husks, banana peels, and sponges, which played havoc with drainage.

John discovered that, by unblocking sewer lines, he could make a significant amount of money in a short time with relatively little effort. Because it was such filthy work, he would only undertake this terrible task when he was drunk. Since he was regularly drunk, this became a standing profession.

In addition to being inebriated, unblocking sewers required John to lower himself into a cement manhole about eight feet deep and three feet in diameter. Once at the bottom, John would take a rod, or a long firm wire, and work the line, poking and twisting until it opened. He never used gloves, since they quickly became sopped and only got in the way. To ensure it was flowing properly, water would be poured from the manhole through the pipe, and someone at the riverside two hundred yards away would watch to see that it exited. This task would typically take less than half an hour, for which John would earn 2,000 shillings ($20), the equivalent of eight full day's work for a casual laborer.

When he was down on his luck, John would sometimes connive to block the sewer himself. First, he would find a plastic bottle that precisely fit the diameter of a sewer line. Then he'd attach the bottle to a long rod and, at night, sneak down to the river and force it up one of the sewer pipes. After a few days, the line would back up, the residents would complain, and the landlord would run to find John. John would drop into the manhole, feign some maneuvers, and eventually make his way to the riverbank. There, he'd smear himself with some filth so that he appeared to be hard at work. Then he'd grab the rod and pull with all his might; and as a septic sommelier, he'd gracefully uncork the effluent line. Heroically marching up the bank, he'd collect a cool 2,000 shillings ($20), which would keep him in drink for the next short while.

Chapter 15
FROM DESERT DEW TO JAIL

Victor Maregwa was a good friend who John had known for many years in Good Samaritan. In 1993, Victor, one year younger than John, and his sister, Margaret Muthoni (who became John's girlfriend), joined the orphanage when their mother died of AIDS. After John was thrown out of the orphanage at the end of 2002, he lost touch with Victor. By chance, they met up again in Eastleigh in 2006, when they were ferrying people in handcarts across muddy streets during the rainy season. Always friendly with each other, they decided to rent a room together in Eastleigh. For the next two years, they supported each other through a continual series of odd jobs.

From the time he'd been in Good Samaritan, Victor had held fast to the vision that he would not be on the streets for long. He was critical of the lifestyle on the streets and would frequently

chide John for his habits: "You're smoking too much bhang."
"If you keep up drinking that way, where will you be in ten years?"

Although initially annoyed by this nagging, John had to admit
to himself that Victor was a great friend who talked sense.

One night in 2006, John and Victor decided to go out for
a drink. At six thirty, they parked themselves at a corner table at
one of Wangu's establishments, the Desert Dew, located on 10th
Street in the heart of Eastleigh. Wangu chose this name because she
made most of the money from her dens in the very late night and
early morning hours. The name Desert Dew was redolent of the
precious moisture that forms on desert plants during these same
early morning hours after a rare rainfall.

At ten thirty, five policemen burst into the Desert Dew, not
surprised to find everyone drunk. This squad of cops had just
started that beat that night but had not been given the word from
the OCS to pass over the Desert Dew. Angrily, the head patrolman
banged on the server's table, grabbed a bottle of changa'a, and
demanded of the nonplussed pour meister: "Is this what you
serve here?"

Before an answer was forthcoming, the drunken crowd started
to jeer the police, hurling foul insults in their mother tongues. The
incensed officers started slapping the customers. Because it was
now clear that everyone was consuming illegal alcohol, the police
ordered all to stand and display their national ID cards over their
heads. They were then handcuffed in pairs, and when the irons ran
out, those who remained unfettered were forced to tie their shirts
together. The officers then attempted to herd the rowdy mob to the
station. Everyone was so drunk, however, that the uncouth rabble

stumbled about a hundred yards down the street until the police finally gave up and called for vans to haul them away.

John and Victor, along with the rest of the troop, were jailed at the police station in the adjacent Pangani neighborhood. Before entering the cell block, everyone was required to empty his pockets and leave one shoe outside the main gate so he could not easily run away.

As they entered the block, John saw forty men packed into an eight-foot-by-ten-foot cell. He later learned that they had been caught disturbing the peace, a serious offense in authoritarian Kenya. His group from the bar numbered only fifteen. They were escorted to another cell in which there were no blankets or furnishings of any kind. They took turns sleeping on the floor huddled together. There was no toilet; nor was there hygienic paper. However, they were privileged to have two large buckets in which to relieve themselves. Now and then, each would get a thermos of water to clean himself. Worst of all, though, were the ticks, which the prisoners picked off each other like baboons.

It was hard for John to be in jail without alcohol. But as friends came to visit, they would slip John money to bribe the guards to bring in alcohol and bhang.

Victor, John, and the other patrons sat in jail for two weeks. They were never formally charged, never brought to court, and never appeared before a judge. After performing various menial tasks around the station—sweeping floors, cleaning windows, cutting the grass—they were released to walk out the front door. They later learned that they had received relatively privileged treatment because Wangu had vehemently complained to the

OCS that her license was current, and her establishment had been improperly raided. Remorsefully, the OCS admitted the mistake but said he could not simply release her customers, since they had to serve some time as examples for other prisoners. He assured her, however, that he had given them a spacious cell, light duties, two buckets, and an early release.

* * *

Although Kiumane offered John a stable residence and job, living in a changa'a den was too much of a temptation for someone who already had a taste for alcohol. Almost everyone in Mathare without a steady job was an alcoholic—and that was a high percentage of the inhabitants. Men were mostly given to drink, but there were also some ladies who frequented the dens, usually with their boyfriends or husbands, some by themselves. Those on their own were typically alcoholics looking for men to buy them drinks. Some were hookers whose charges depended on how much alcohol the prospective client would purchase for her. Plentiful drink could reduce the price of services to as little as twenty shillings.

For John, it was not simply the ready availability of alcohol that led to his addiction, it was the pervasive desire to forget his circumstances and numb his emotions. He carried the burden of despair, a cloud that never cleared. No matter how hard he tried to move forward, it always came to naught. His father had paid no attention to him, his late mother had been consumed in a haze of mental illness and drink, his aunts had disowned him, and even Mama Mercy had turned on him and the others at the end of secondary school.

Whenever he thought of the sad events in his life, he reached for a glass. But he was not a solitary drunk; John was too gregarious to isolate himself. Rather, he always wanted to be around people who were drinking. He enjoyed hearing their stories and enjoyed telling his tales. He felt it made life easier; it made life go faster.

Sadly, his persistent drinking came at a terrible price. Although he had been thrown out of Good Samaritan at the end of 2002, he had maintained close contact with Margaret Muthoni, his girlfriend of ten years. Since Kiumane was only about a hundred yards from the orphanage, John made sure to meet up with Margaret every morning to walk her to St. Theresa's Girls Secondary School along the Juja Road. Every evening, he'd be sure to escort her home.

By 2004, however, John had sunk into alcoholism and supported himself principally through his work in the sewers. One afternoon, he met Margaret on her way home. She smelled something funny on him, like alcohol. He insisted that he had just been to the barber, and it was only a strong aftershave lotion. The next day, they met again. She detected the same aroma, and he tried the same excuse. Hardly believing that he had been to the barber twice on successive days, she now knew he had been drinking. Margaret dumped John on the spot. She said she loved him, but she could not continue spending her life with a drunkard who lied to her.

John became known as a "DDO," a daily drinking officer as they called those in Mathare who are drunk every day. In his darkest moments, he came to believe there was nothing to do but drink and die in Mathare. He thought to himself, *There is nothing but me and changa'a.*

Chapter 16
CHE MATHARE VIDEO SHOP

Toward the end of 2006, the CHE Mathare Youth Group approached Mama Mercy to ask permission to construct a small building on her property on the opposite side of the street from Good Samaritan. The group was comprised of some thirty-five youth aged sixteen to twenty-five who lived on the south side of Mathare. Many had been raised in Good Samaritan, and John knew all the members.

Most of the group had failed to complete secondary school and together had formed a service organization that would provide them a modest income while supporting the community. The initials CHE stood for "Clean Health and Education." Barclays Bank donated several handcarts, with which the group planned to provide much needed regular garbage collection and water distribution throughout the area. When not in use, the carts could be rented out. Now, they wanted to construct a video entertainment center and small headquarters office. Mama Mercy was delighted to rent them a strip of her property.

Knowing that John was always in need of work, one of the members asked him to help with the construction. Since several sewer lines ran through the plot, the group knew John was familiar with the conduits. And besides, he could tolerate the foul smell. He dug postholes for the vertical uprights, earning twenty shillings per boring. He also went to the supply shop with the carpenter and pulled the cart loaded with materials. The group engaged him in almost every task but one—they would never trust him with money. John had the reputation as a *manyweti* (drunkard) and the concern was that he would pilfer the construction funds to purchase changa'a. The group was astute.

When construction was complete, the video shop was a fifteen-foot-by-twenty-five-foot tin and cardboard shack built on the slope down to the Mathare River, which afforded viewers naturally tiered theatre seating. At the lower end of the sloping room atop a battered table sat a widescreen TV. Seating for thirty was a jumbled menagerie of two-person wooden benches and cracked plastic and bent steel chairs. A small eight-foot-by-ten-foot room was added to the side as a sleeping quarters for members. Although John was permitted to sleep in the shop, he had to crash in the viewing section because he was not a member.

From early 2006 when the building was completed until the end of 2008, John moved between Kiumane and the video shop. Most of the time was spent at Kiumane, but the video shop provided him a place to sleep. He much preferred sleeping in the shop, since he wouldn't be bothered by drunks, and best of all, there were no lice.

Every morning, he'd sweep the rubbish from the previous night's theatre patrons, sprinkle some water on the floor, and mop up. It was important for the room to be especially presentable on Sundays, when a congregation of the African Independent Church rented the space for their worship service.

At that time, few residents of Mathare could afford a satellite hookup, and there certainly was no cable service in the slums, so the video shop did a brisk business. The most popular films were action movies—Bruce Lee being the top attraction. Nigerian cinema was also a big draw. Films were shown in DVD format. Their inventory was procured through DJs in the Central Business District, who had access to a wide variety of cut-rate disks.

After the shop began to prosper, they installed a satellite dish, mainly used to beam in sports events, especially live European soccer matches. The day's offerings were displayed on a sandwich board that sat street side. One of John's tasks was to keep the board current. Prices varied according to the popularity of the show. Movies might be as little as five shillings. The price of football matches varied from thirty to fifty shillings, with the better clubs commanding the higher price.

Although CHE Mathare had a community service focus, the group also knew what sold. So eventually they began offering porn flicks for late-night viewing. This was highly risky, since pornography was illegal in Kenya. So, precautions had to be taken. First, the movies were never publically advertised on the street sign. Instead, musical groups, such as UB40, would be posted on the placard. Artists such as Jose Chameleone with his Afrobeat from Uganda and Diamond Platnumz with Bongo Hip Hop from Tanzania were also announced. Locals in the know, however, were aware what this really meant.

For most regular films, the sound would be loud enough to hear on the street, a simple way of drawing attention to the shop. But the sultry soundtracks for the illegal films would be turned off, and the music of the advertised group would be piped to the street. The price of porn films was fifty shillings, the same as topflight football clubs. No doubt, Manchester United and FC Barcelona would be delighted to know that, in addition to their numerous sporting triumphs, their matches commanded the same top price in Mathare as low-grade porn flicks.

This aggressive programming, however, occasionally got CHE Mathare in trouble. Policemen on patrol were always keen to shake down miscreants. In order to guard against unwanted intrusion when screening erotica, the main entrance from the street was dead bolted from the inside, reinforced with an iron bar propped against the back of the door, which was then planted in the floor. When the unmistakable loud knock and menacing voice of a patrolman made itself known, the audience and projectionist would empty out the back door, scurrying down the sloping pasture toward the river. Once all had escaped, John's job was to open the door and let in the officers.

Since these films were typically shown late at night, John was usually drunk by then and often asleep. The commotion would wake him, but he knew exactly what to do—play drunk, for which he was always prepared. After extensive banging and loud threatening shouts, John would walk to the door and let the police enter. Summoning his best acting skills, he'd immediately stumble and fall onto his mattress. They'd pick him up, slap him around, and even try to hold him up, but John played dishrag and fell limp to the floor. Concluding that he was too drunk to be watching the film, they'd give him a kick and leave.

* * *

During these years of alcoholic oblivion, John had a strong sense of bravado. Often, he would shout as he scuttled along Mathare's crowded streets. Wherever John went, people knew he was there. He felt the inflated sense that, when he was drunk, the world belonged to him.

He felt like a millionaire, thinking to himself, *I can sleep as late as I want because I don't have to go to work. I work for myself and myself alone—no one can fire me. Sure, I'm not sleeping on a fine mattress. I sleep wrapped in polyethylene papers. But as they say, "No matter where you sleep, you've slept."*[5] *I eat every day for free, and I can get clothes whenever I want.*

He'd clothe himself by employing one of his well-practiced pranks. When he needed new clothing, he figured he'd do housewives a favor and "unhang" clothes from their lines. If they caught him wearing an article they recognized, he'd challenge them, snorting brazenly, "Do you really think this is the only shirt like this that the company manufactured? And, by the way, where is your name on this shirt?" If all else failed, John would resort to the age-old defiance of a true scoundrel—possession is nine-tenths of the law: "This may have been your shirt, but it's my shirt now!"

---

[5] A proverbial Swahili saying

As John moved between Kiumane and the video shop, he'd pass in front of Good Samaritan. Still harboring deep animosity toward Mama Mercy, every night at eleven o'clock, he'd issue a loud yell directly in front of the blue gate. It would start with an ascending screech and end with a rude expression—"eeeeeeeeeeeeEEEEEEEEEEE ... Kino" (Bitch)! It was so loud that it could clearly be heard on the other side of the river. Yet because the expression was in the Kamba language, few residents knew what it meant. Mama Mercy didn't speak Kamba, but she knew it was directed at her.

Chapter 17
A COCKROACH BUYS DINNER

Now and then, all of us need to treat ourselves to something special. When one is just scraping by, as street boys do, that little bit of luxury can be hard to come by. But just as a little skullduggery earned John a couple of thousand shillings for unblocking sewers, so sheer brass occasionally bought him a good meal. How to do so was virtually a science, which John was delighted to teach others.

It starts with dressing in your finest clothes and picking the right establishment. A street boy must select a restaurant that's not in his territory, so no one will know him. Of course, he doesn't have enough money to pay for a decent meal, perhaps with only sixty shillings in his pocket, which is already spoken for—fifty for glue and ten for cigarettes. But that doesn't stop him from walking confidently into a hotel and taking a seat.

Choosing a table must be done carefully. It's best to be in a corner, but close enough to other diners so they can overhear you. There can't be anyone behind you; the other patrons, the waiter and cashier must all be in front of you, so you can clearly see them. If the seat you need is not available, then be patient until it comes open; after all, you're now a discriminating diner.

After you've politely placed your order with the waiter, you call him back and ask for a nice hearty soup. You enjoy your meal slowly, savoring with refinement. As you are finishing your plate, you observe the others nearby to make sure no one is watching. When all is clear, you reach into your pocket, remove a cockroach, which you killed just before entering the premises, and mix it into some of the food left on your plate.

Now you summon the waiter and request a glass of water. When he returns, you take another helping of food in which you are sure to include the dead insect. Pause and look up at the waiter to make sure he has witnessed this culinary travesty. Of course, the waiter will be astonished and embarrassed.

Now it's time to feign disgust and cause a scene. In a voice just loud enough for nearby tables to hear clearly but not too dramatically, you emphatically ask, "Is this what you serve here? Cockroaches?"

Other guests will naturally turn their heads to see what's going on.

At this point, the waiter will do almost anything to keep you calm and your voice low. Most often, he will offer not to charge you for the meal if you leave immediately. To conclude the prank successfully, you comply with the waiter's request, departing with an air of disgust, spiced with a pinch of condescension just thick enough to mask your inner glee.

This maneuver is best performed on public holidays when restaurants offer their finest fare.

Chapter 18
THIEF FOR A WEEK

A common belief held by many street boys was that most thieves enjoyed expensive, luxurious lifestyles. They could steal a phone, sell it for 10,000 shillings ($100), and then buy fancy shoes. The best-dressed street boys were always thieves. But the other side of the coin was that thieves often ended up dead.

In Western society, theft and armed robbery are serious criminal offenses for which jail time is served. In Kenya, theft is also a serious crime. But it is often adjudicated by street justice, with the punishment being death administered by a mob of outraged citizens. A common form of punishment is "necklacing," in which an old tire is dropped around the neck and torso and then lit on fire. It is a gruesome death, and the victim wishes for someone with a firearm to administer a coup de grâce. Police rarely intervene. Rather, they let those whose property has been stolen mete out justice.

* * *

John knew Elvis Nyabochwa from the short time they'd spent together at Good Samaritan. Elvis's father was a matatu conductor on Route 6 in Eastleigh. When Elvis's mother died of AIDS, his father brought him to the orphanage. After a short time, Elvis left Good Samaritan, unhappy with the disciplined routine and attracted to the highlife he fancied that thieves enjoyed.

One morning, John and Elvis ran into each other on the streets of Mathare. Elvis had two friends with him who John did not know. Elvis explained that they were going to pull off a robbery, and they needed a fourth person. He asked John to join them. John had never considered such a thing; it was dangerous and wrong. Elvis kept pressing; he needed that fourth person. Giving into peer pressure, John finally agreed.

The callow gang made its way to the bus stage at 1st Avenue and 12th Street, a major roundabout in Eastleigh, where they planned to target wealthy Somalis alighting from matatus. They were feeling particularly bold, since they were hopped up on bhang, and one of Elvis's friends was carrying a gun.

As a well-dressed gentleman and his lady walked from a bus, the four mugged them, taking their expensive cell phones and some cash. Rather than recoil in fear, the man angrily advanced toward the boys and shouted that, if they wanted the rest of his money, they'd have to kill him on the spot.

Terrified at such a brazen confrontation, the boys turned and ran down the busy sidewalks of 1st Avenue. Amazingly, the man followed in pursuit, chasing them all the way to 6th Street.

Turning down 6th Street the boys made for 2nd Avenue, a

broad, potholed dirt road with fewer cars and pedestrians, giving them the opportunity to run faster. At 6th Street however, they encountered a police squad patrolling in a Land Cruiser. A rather suspicious scene unfolded before the officers' eyes—four young men running frantically chased by a gentleman in a fine suit. Once he yelled, "Thieves, thieves!" the policemen's hunches were confirmed.

The officers fired up the Land Cruiser and gave pursuit. Deep ruts in the road, however, prevented the officers from catching up to the boys. They dismounted and began firing at the wannabe bandits. Even if they had wanted to engage the police, the boys were no match for the officers' high-powered rifles. Besides, the pistol the one boy carried had all of two bullets.

John felt lead whiz by. He was literally running for his life. Because he was the smallest of the four with the shortest stride, he ran a few yards behind the others, just to the right of Elvis. Suddenly he heard a soft thud as a bullet pierced the back of Elvis's head. Blood spatter covered John's face, arms, and clothes as he passed alongside of Elvis, who toppled like a felled tree.

Because Elvis was carrying the cash and phones, the police stopped the chase when they caught up to him and discovered they had recovered the stolen goods.

Having escaped the police, John ran across the Juja Road to the safer environs of Mathare. Deeply shaken, he cleaned up, changed clothes, and made his way back to see what had happened to his friend.

When he arrived forty-five minutes later, a crowd had surrounded Elvis's motionless body. The police were still on the scene. But with the change of clothes, John was not afraid of being recognized.

Police investigations of shootings in Kenya were handled differently than in the United States. First, because of the prevalence of HIV/AIDS in Africa, and especially in the slums, policemen were reluctant to handle bloody corpses. Instead, they provided latex gloves to street boys, with the understanding that the boys could keep any money they found on the body as long as they turned over all other evidence. The boys were also expected to place the remains into a body bag and load it into the police wagon. Emotionally calloused from being constantly high and always impoverished, street boys were overjoyed to assist.

The police also used shootings as an opportunity to stage a spectacle for the community. Not only were they sure to boast of their crime-solving acumen, they exploited the horrific event to instill fear and respect for their authority.

After Elvis's body was placed in a van and the crowd dispersed, John saw the Somali gentleman climb into a police car. John figured that, after making an official report, the man would probably recover the phones. But his money was now patrimony of the streets.

Terrified to have been so close to death, John walked solemnly back to the video shop. Several days later, he found Elvis's father working Route 6 and gave him the sad news. In time, the family claimed his body from the city mortuary and buried it in the Langata Cemetery, in one of the countless nondescript graves for Nairobi's poor.

Thus, John decided to end his brief life of larceny.

PART IV

RENEWAL

——— 2009-2013 ———

Every achievement, every step forward comes from courage, from cleanliness with respect to yourself.

—Friedrich Nietzsche

Chapter 19
IF I CAN'T BE A LAWYER, I'LL BE A FARMER

It was December 2008, coming up on John's twenty-fifth birthday. As usual, he was in a bar drinking. Suddenly, he heard large vehicles trundle by. He thought it might be the police, so he went outside to look. Two vans had pulled up in front of Good Samaritan and parked by the new cowsheds opposite the blue entrance gate. Two white ladies got out. John felt the urge to go over and have a chat. Mama Mercy met the ladies. Kay was the leader of the team.

While Kay and Mercy were conversing, John stumbled up and interrupted. "Hi, I'm John. How are you?" he slurred.

Mama tried to shoo him away, but John persisted.

Unprompted, he mumbled, "I was one of the guys who started this place, and she chased me away."

Kay turned to Mercy, puzzled, "Who is this?"

John jumped in with the answer. "I was the first one here."

Kay, a veteran of many trips to the slums, was not put off. She turned and asked John his name.

"I'm John Maina. I'm the one who came to this home first in 1991, but Mama Mercy chased us away."

By now thoroughly annoyed, Mercy glared at John and in Swahili told him to go away, get back to his drink, and she would give him some food later. Mama turned back to Kay and related her version of the story: John had been a very good student, but he'd left school and turned to drink.

Kay was a professor at an American university and a longtime benefactress of Good Samaritan. She had been our superb tour guide on the first trip Linda and I had taken to East Africa in 2001. Since then, she had founded her own nonprofit organization, which, among other projects, raised money for tuition for children at Good Samaritan. Kay was making her annual visit and had some good news to deliver to Mama Mercy. Not only had she brought her usual gift of food, she had also gathered donations to fund college tuition for six older members of the orphanage.

Able to discern opportunity through all of the histrionics, Kay asked John, "Would you like to go back to school? If you would, come back tomorrow at two o'clock, and we'll talk about it."

John went back to the club and resumed drinking, excessively. His curious friends asked him why he was talking to the *mzungu* (white foreign) lady. He was unable to respond; he couldn't remember any of the conversation.

About two o'clock the next afternoon, a boy from Good Samaritan came into the club and shook John, who was still passed out from the binge the night before. "Why have you been drinking when the mzungu is trying to help you?" the boy asked.

As he stammered to consciousness, John couldn't remember talking to anyone yesterday. John always needed to anesthetize his deep emotional wounds, even when opportunity presented itself.

"Come on. Get up. Get going," the boy insisted. "She wants to talk to you."

Feeling queasy, John stumbled out the pub and made his way down the street to Good Samaritan, where Kay was waiting.

She commented that he looked chipper and that he didn't seem so drunk. She asked why he was better.

"Because I don't have any money in my pocket to buy more drink."

Undeterred by the waggish remark, she asked, "Do you remember what we talked about yesterday?"

"Not really. I was too drunk."

"Well, yesterday we talked about your story, and now I want to talk to *you*." She went on to explain that her organization had raised money to send some of the older youth who had grown up in Good Samaritan to technical college. Kay was aware that John had received an overall score of "C–" on his secondary school exams, which placed him in the top 30 percent of all students. Scores of "A" and "B" were necessary to enter university. A "C" qualified one for technical college.

Still under the influence, John arrogantly insisted, "Yes, I'd like to go, but not to a day college. I want to go to a boarding school."

Patiently, Kay explained that she had retained several slots at an agricultural college in Limuru in lush rural highlands about fifteen miles outside of Nairobi. John presumptuously accepted her offer, then gruffly turned and walked away.

Beneath his crass behavior lay a deep longing. Later that day as he composed himself, John thought, *I really wanted to be somebody—just somebody—but my dreams were cut short. My dreams of being a judge or lawyer have been ruined. But if I can't be what I wanted to be, maybe I can be something else. I wanted to be a judge or a lawyer, but if I go to agriculture school, I'll become a very good farmer. All I want is to be able to depend on myself.*

* * *

The next day, Kay took John and the other candidates on a shopping spree to outfit them for school. They were equipped with uniforms, shoes, and a large metal box in which to keep their belongings. As the day wound down, Kay explained that she would not be able to drive out to Limuru with them tomorrow but that she would send a driver to pick them up bright and early.

Chapter 20
BAKED GOODS, JUICES, MAIZE, AND DAIRY

Tired and badly hung over again, John fell on the road up the hill to the Esso station, where the driver was waiting to take the new students to Limuru. John passed out as soon as he got into the bus. He didn't see that his old friend, Gitari, had come by. A few years ago, Gitari had moved to another Nairobi slum, Mukuru kwa Ruben, and they hadn't seen each other since then. Gitari had gotten the news of John's good fortune to attend college, and he'd faithfully come by Good Samaritan to see him off with best wishes. But John was unavailable.

John had to be awakened once they arrived at the college. Limuru Agricultural Youth Centre was located on the slopes of rolling, verdant fields far into the countryside, with no other buildings in sight. John had only once been out of the city of Nairobi—to attend the drama festival in Kisumu. This was an all-new world. The campus was beautiful, with solid, impressive structures set amid lush lawns and towering trees—greenery never seen in Mathare. Beyond the entrance was a long, narrow parking lot, around which were three buildings—to the right, the administration block; to the left, the building where he would take classes; and, at the end, the large dining and assembly hall.

Limuru Tech was the best thing that had happened to John since he had been in secondary school six years ago. Besides offering him the opportunity to get on a professional track, the school environment inspired him to stop drinking and smoking. On arrival at the college, the students were bundled off to the assembly hall, where they were greeted by faculty and staff. Each student was asked two questions. When they came to John it was obvious that he was drunk. The two questions were: Why are you drunk? And will you stop drinking? He didn't answer the first question but committed in front of all present to the second.

At the college, students selected one of four professional streams: mechanics, entrepreneurship, computers, or food processing. Wanting to acquire practical skills but not mechanically inclined or interested in computers, John chose to pursue food processing.

The food-processing curriculum covered four areas of food preparation—baked goods, juices, maize, and dairy. In the baking segment, students practiced preparing chapati and mandazis in bulk, which they would then serve to the rest of the student body at mealtimes. In the maize segment, they learned how to turn raw kernels into flour of various consistencies. Sieves of different apertures would be placed beneath the grinder to capture the multiple grades of flour.

In the dairy chapter, students learned how to separate butter from milk. At Limuru, they used centrifugal machines; other colleges used an electric apparatus. In the juices course, students first learned the theory of processing drinks from raw fruits and later took field trips to JKUAT (Jomo Kenyatta University of Agriculture and Technology) and KIST (Kenya Institute of Science and Technology) to learn how to operate the most modern processing machines.

As he settled into the classroom setting, John's addictions were obvious to his instructors. Two teachers walked him to sobriety. Miss Akol, his food-processing instructor, approached him during the first few days in class, when she saw him sweating and unable to hold his pen. Embarrassed, John asked to speak with her privately outside the classroom. When she learned he was going through alcohol and nicotine withdrawal, she gave him twenty shillings and told him to go to a local kiosk to buy some cigarettes. She confided in John that she used to smoke twenty each day, so she knew how hard it was to stop. On the street, John was used to smoking two or three each hour. She gave him only enough money to buy four sticks, which she recommended he smoke at 10:00 a.m., after lunch, at 4:00 p.m., and after dinner. He stretched the funds to buy five nonfiltered cigarettes, commonly known as "rockets."

Mr. Macharia, the mechanics instructor, was a smoker and drinker. Although John didn't follow his course of study, Macharia could see John shaking from alcohol withdrawal. He would invite John into his garage office and gave him a few swigs from a flask, which he hid in a toolbox. In the first weeks, Macharia even took John to a local bar and bought him a beer, helping to ease him slowly from his habit.

After about six weeks, John stopped feeling sick and was well on his way to breaking his addictions. He came to love these two teachers because they had taken the time to understand his situation, had not passed judgment, and had worked to get him righted.

After those difficult initial weeks, John settled in and loved the school. After years of wandering the streets, he fell right into the routine:

6:00	Wake up and bathe. Perform daily chores.
7:00	Report to dining hall. Take tea.
8:00	Morning classes
10:30	Tea break
10:45	Classes resume
1:00	Lunch
2:00	Afternoon classes
4:30	Classes end
6:00	Dinner
Evening	Free time: Watch TV, study

There were fifty-two students following the food-processing curriculum, of which four girls and two boys from Good Samaritan were sponsored by Kay. The program was designed as a one-year course of study, followed by a six-month "attachment" (internship), for which the student earned a certificate. After completing this stage, one could continue to earn a diploma, the equivalent of a university degree. Kay had promised that she would provide funding for a diploma for those who performed well in the certificate phase. As he got further into the program, John's heart was set on getting a diploma, hopefully at JKUAT, one of the top schools in its field in Kenya. With that degree in hand, he would be able to work at any number of food-processing companies, maybe even the prestigious Kenya Cereal Board, which prepared many of the basic foodstuffs for the nation's wanachi.

Kay kept careful track of her students in Limuru. Through the driver, who served as Kay's eyes and ears on the ground, she received biweekly reports on the students' progress. She made sure they had proper clothing and ample school supplies. She was particularly keen to follow John, since she had taken some risk in sponsoring such a controversial, wayward young man. Occasionally, Miss Akol would speak directly with Kay by phone, proudly reporting how John had conquered his addictions and had become one of the top students in the program.

Once sober, John performed superbly. In addition to one's main course of study, every student had to take classes in entrepreneurship, covering basic management and business skills. In 2009, John was honored as the top student in entrepreneurship and was given an award at an all-school assembly. He was an example of how the ingenuity of living on the street translated into business acumen.

Down a gentle slope behind the administration block were the dormitory buildings for the boys and girls. John's room was the size of a large walk-in closet with two built-in bunk beds immediately inside the door to the right. Beyond the beds was a closet divided horizontally into upper and lower halves for each boarder. At the far end, beneath a small window was a table and chair. John liked the room, mainly because it was right next door to the community washrooms. He also liked his roommate, Julius Karume, a Kikuyu from nearby Limuru Town who studied mechanics.

Over the course of the first several weeks, John observed that students were throwing leftover food into a garbage can. At an all-school assembly John raised his hand, walked to the front, and addressed the entire student body. He was enraged that his classmates were throwing food into the garbage cans—not just food scraps but whole chicken legs and half sandwiches. He threatened to fight anyone he saw throwing food away. He fumed, "This is unholy. I used to eat out of garbage cans. How dare anyone waste like this?"

Although somewhat put off by John's aggressive belligerence, the principal asked John to show him the refuse bin. John took him to the barrel on the walk from the dining hall to the dormitories. Sure enough, they discovered far too much perfectly good food. At the next assembly, the principal thanked John for raising this issue and admonished all students to modulate their portions and take from the meal line only what they could consume. At the following assembly one month later, the principal thanked students for the noticeable improvement.

As the first year of classroom and practicum came to an end, it was time for John to arrange an attachment. In Kenya, it was the student's personal responsibility to land his own assignment. The school supplied letters explaining the significance of the attachment and vouching for student's bona fides, but it was the student who had to shop the market. To land a position, John returned to

Nairobi in December 2009. One of his friends was working as a security guard at the Kuguru Food Complex in one of the large industrial parks just outside the Central Business District. The operation had been launched in 1988 by the Kuguru family. The firm specialized in beverages and maize products, food-processing operations John had studied. In January 2010, having just turned twenty-six years old, John passed the interview process and began work in the Kuguru maize flour unit.

Standard procedure for interns in Kenya was to receive half pay, for which they were expected to work only half the hours of a regular employee. If the workday formally began at 7:30 a.m., the intern would be allowed to arrive at 8:30 a.m. and could leave at 2:30 to 3:00p.m., while the staff might not finish until 5:00 p.m. An additional advantage of attachments was that the interns were permitted to float between operating units to broaden their experience.

From the first day, John was captivated by his job. Rather than take advantage of the option of shorter hours, he stayed even longer than the regular employees, arriving before 7:00 a.m. and leaving after 5:00 p.m. He was hungry to learn. He could see that this was the ticket to a middle-class lifestyle. He had just completed the first year at a well-respected technical college and was now slotting into the managerial track at a topflight company. A bright future was in sight!

Chapter 21
PANGAS!

John started his attachment in January 2010, immediately after the classroom phase in Limuru had ended. Moving back to Nairobi, John took a room in Mathare across the river from Good Samaritan. Kuguru Food Complex was five and a half miles and three bus lines away. But Mathare was John's home, and he knew many people at that end of the valley.

The Mathare slum lies in a narrow valley spanning both sides of the river. There is only one main street on each side. Perched along these streets are the rows of kiosks, which make up the neighborhood's dynamic small merchant trade. Many shopkeepers live in the back of their tiny kiosks in a space not much bigger than a closet. Behind this row of shops are other makeshift habitations. As Mathare is a community that originally began as an informal settlement, nothing is neatly arranged there. A warren of narrow, winding footpaths forms a maze of shacks. Many are one-room quarters partitioned by a sheet to create two spaces—the living room, with kitchenware in the corner, and the bedroom. Cardboard, tin, and heavy plastic make up the walls, while corrugated galvanized metal ("gal sheets") form the roof. These units are packed next to each other with no gap in between and cover most of the terrain down to the banks of the river. The only open spaces are those in which shallow trenches have been cut by running water, usually through a combination of rain runoff and leaking sewer mains. Litter is everywhere in the slums, and discarded plastic shopping bags flutter about. As the bags drape themselves along the sides of foul gutters, they form the appearance of multicolored candle wax dripping into the crevice. More than the pervasive stench, the atmosphere is permeated with the stink of wretchedness, of want, of desperation.

Leaving work after 7:00 p.m. meant that John returned to Mathare after darkness had fallen. Dropped by a matatu at the abandoned petrol station along the Juja Road, John descended the slope toward the main street on the south bank. Instead of turning right onto the thoroughfare and walking a hundred yards to Good Samaritan, he'd veer to the left and slipped through a small passageway next to Kiumane. Beyond the shack, the well-beaten path opened to a twenty-foot long clearing created by a two-foot deep waxen trench. Each night, John would make his way by dim ambient light down to the river, across a rickety footbridge, and up the other side to his room.

In mid-February, six weeks after his attachment began, John was coming home at about nine o'clock. Sitting outside Kiumane were five boys who had grown up with John at Good Samaritan. They were teenagers now, about ten years younger than John. They had left the home, unable to abide by Mama Mercy's strict rules. Out on the streets, they supported themselves by petty theft. They knew John was now in college, which meant to them that he had money.

As he passed, one of the guys shouted to John to give him a "tip." John told them that he had nothing, which was pretty much true since all he had was fifty shillings for the next day's bus fare. The boys wouldn't accept John's rebuff.

"Don't tell us that. We know you're working."

"Stop being stupid," John parried. "If I had it, I'd give it to you."

As he walked toward the river, they followed and persisted in asking for money. John tried again to verbally block them. "My friends, I have nothing. Leave me alone."

Followed by the urchins, John tramped down the slope. Just then, a *mzee* (a distinguished elder gentleman) was coming up the hill. His phone rang; it was his wife asking where he was. Two boys ran past John to the old man, insolently demanding that he get off the phone so they could use it. Before the mzee could respond, one boy grabbed the phone and reached into the old man's pockets, coming up with 200 shillings. The mzee pleaded with them to return his phone; they could keep the money, but his phone was very important to him.

After robbing the gentleman, they turned to John and vehemently demanded money.

Losing patience, John raised his voice and shouted, "Stop disturbing me."

With that, one of them, Kalenbe, hit John.

John was shocked. "Kalenbe, how can you do this to me?"

"You are stupid," replied the fifteen-year-old. "You didn't give us a tip, and yet we used to sit at the hotel and drink together. We used to share all we had, and now you're refusing to give us a tip."

The site where John was attacked

John became angry. A young kid like this couldn't be allowed to hit him. So, John hit Kalenbe, knocking him into the watery ditch. Another boy lunged at John, who wrestled him into the ditch as well.

Relieved that he had dispatched the ruffians, John continued walking down the slope toward the river into the uncertain darkness.

Then he heard them coming. This time they were carrying pool cues, *jembes* (hoes), and *pangas* (machetes). It was clear they meant business. Now he realized he had made a big mistake by refusing to give them a mere fifty shillings, but it was too late. He grabbed one of the jembes away from a youth and started swinging wildly at them. Then they shone a flashlight directly into John's eyes, blinding him.

Next, he felt a machete blow striking him along the side of his head, cutting his ear and cheek. Blood spewed all over. A second blow came across the other side, piercing his lower jaw and lip—more blood.

Then he heard Kalenbe scream, "See what you made me do—drink this filthy water." With that, Kalenbe swung his panga with all his might straight at the crown of John's head. John saw the shiny steel blade reflected in the flashlight beam. Immediately he raised his forearm, blocking the full force of the potentially lethal blow but cutting into the tendons and lacerating his skull from back to front.

Hit three times, with blood pouring from his head, John began to feel weak and fell into the ditch. Apparently triumphant, one boy shouted, "Leave him. He was pretending to be strong. Now we've sent him to God."

John lay in the ditch for about ten minutes. Finally, he mustered enough strength to begin crawling on his knees up the hill toward the main street. The boys, who had not dispersed, saw him. One shouted in amazement, "He's not gone yet!" They attacked John again with cues and started beating him.

Just then, one of John's old friends from Good Samaritan, Steven Kamigi, was coming down the path. He was an accomplished thief and carried a gun. As he approached the violent scene, he asked what was the matter.

One of the boys bragged, "This guy thinks he's strong, but he doesn't know we're the heroes in this area."

"'Who is he?" asked Kamigi.

Wiping the blood from his eyes, John uttered faintly, "Kamigi, it's Maina."

Instinctively knowing what had happened, Kamigi shouted to the boys, "How dare you try to fool me? It's Maina, and you know it." Kamigi immediately pulled his pistol and shot one of the boys in the knee. The others scattered.

As best John could, he explained to Kamigi what happened. Kamigi knew that John urgently needed help and dragged him a hundred yards to the front gate of Good Samaritan. He told John he had to leave else he'd be accused of the assault. So Kamigi dropped John and ran.

Growing weaker and weaker, John did his best to cry out. "Mama, I'm hurt. Mama Mercy help." He banged on the metal door, causing as much racket as he could.

Finally, a girl who had come down to use the bathroom heard him and yelled, "Mama, Mama, it's Maina. He's bleeding badly."

Mercy came, took one look, and then summoned a driver from the neighborhood to take John to the hospital. That was the last thing he remembered.

Chapter 22
IN A HOSPITAL NEAR NAIROBI

After the driver picked him up, John lost consciousness on the ride to the hospital. He lay in a coma for three days. When he awoke, the first thing he saw were curtains bearing the letters "KDH." He tried to make sense of them. Then he realized he was bandaged, with intravenous lines running to his arm. Slowly it occurred to him that he was in a hospital—Kiambu District Hospital—about nine miles from Good Samaritan.

As he painfully turned his wounded head, he saw a glorious site—his sister, Jane, sitting at his bedside. A weak smile glowed faintly, undetected through the heavy bandages. A neighbor had told her of the attack the morning after it happened and that a driver had rushed John to the Kiambu hospital. As soon as she'd heard, Jane had rushed to be with him. She had seen him bandaged on the head and mouth, with his lower right arm and hand fully wrapped. For three days she'd cried while he lay unconscious. At the time, Jane had two young children. One was in school; the other she carried with her to the hospital. Because she had almost no money, she had walked the entire distance with the baby tied on her back. It took five hours, but for her, it was no problem; she wanted to be with her brother. John only vaguely recalled that she told him she had been sleeping in the hospital room and that she'd gone home only once to look in on her husband and their other son.

Although John had regained consciousness, it took another two days for him to get his bearings. A doctor helped orient him, asking basic questions such as his name, his age, and what schools and college he had attended. John told her he was studying food processing in Limuru and then incongruously lapsed into an explanation of how he had learned to make yogurt. Next week, the kindly doctor brought him a liter of yogurt, which she had made from his extemporaneous recipe.

When he had stabilized and regained cognition, the doctors spoke with John about his injuries. John had sustained multiple long, deep cuts across the top of his head, along both cheeks and ears, to his mouth, and above his right wrist.

Dr. Mohammed, the ER surgeon who had attended to John, joked, "You must have a metallic head, or God really loves you." More seriously, Dr. Mohammed said that he had seen many machete attacks, which almost no one survived. The wound across the crown of John's head was especially deep but had not pierced the skull or injured the brain. Had John not blocked that blow with his arm, he surely would have died.

* * *

A couple of weeks later, one of the boys who had attacked John paid him a visit. He brought a bag containing a watermelon, some oranges, and mangoes. He explained that the boys were sorry for what they had done and asked him to accept the fruit. John said little, simply replying that what they had done was not God's plan; else he would have died. The boy quietly left the bag and departed.

Shortly afterward, the attending physician stopped and asked John who the visitor was. When he explained that it was one the assailants, the doctor gave a start. She told him not to eat any of it. They had already tried to kill him once. Who knows if they'd poisoned this fruit. With that, she grabbed the bag and promptly disposed of the entire contents.

A few days later, some of John's friends visited him. They insisted that, when he was released, they should round up the perps and take them to the police. Still in pain and without much energy, John was not inclined to pursue their idea.

But his friends had their own designs. In March, Jane delivered the news. The boys started with a visit to the mzee. They were suspicious of him, since he had left the violent scene physically unscathed; they wanted to hear his story. After listening to the old man's version, they asked him menacingly if he had known that Maina was dying. The old man was silent. After they left, the mzee feared that John's friends thought he had set up the attack. Knowing the arbitrary and brutal manner of street justice, he wrote a short letter to his wife and then hung himself from a crossbeam in their room. The innocent old man was buried while John was still in the hospital.

John spent four months in Kiambu District Hospital, from February through June. Jane saw him almost every day. She would come for morning visiting hours and then retire to the lawn, where she'd eat lunch and take a nap. She'd return for the afternoon visitation. Whenever she had a little extra money, she'd leave John a few shillings so he could purchase a small container of milk.

John's half brother, Daniel, used to visit occasionally. It seemed to John that he came more out of social appearance than out of brotherly love. Daniel would come twice each week, always arriving just before visiting hours ended at 5:00 p.m. He'd bring a piece of fruit, spend five to ten minutes with John, and then be on his way.

John and Daniel had not seen much of each other for nearly ten years. Daniel had graduated from secondary school in 2001, one year before John. He'd attained a superb "B+" score on the national exams. Rather than go on to university, however, Daniel had joined Jamii Bora, one of Kenya's premier microfinance operations. He'd lived in Mathare for a few months and had quickly advanced through the ranks. He soon moved to the Kasarani estate, a middle-class community north of Nairobi.

In 2004, Daniel hooked up with the US Army, volunteering to work at supply bases in Afghanistan. He returned after three years with lots of stories and a hefty bank account. Back in Kenya, he purchased two matatu vans licensed to service the Limuru-Nairobi route. Seeing that his brother was struggling, Daniel offered John a job as a conductor on the matatus. The plan was that John would collect fares on the vans and sleep nights at Daniel's home in the beautiful hills of Limuru. For John, it was not even a tempting offer; there was just too much strain over too many years between them. Jane firmly recommended against it, feeling the arrangement could only end badly.

In May 2010, when time came to release John from the hospital, there was bad news. Daniel had spoken with the hospital accountant and learned that the bill was 58,000 shillings ($580), which was far beyond their capacity to pay. Over the course of the next few days, Daniel huddled with the social workers and arranged for payment to be reduced to 8,000 shillings ($80), provided that John stay through the month of June to assist around the hospital. For the next six week then, John fed patients with broken arms, helped those with broken legs to the bathroom, and cleaned the wards.

When it came time to pay the discounted bill, the head doctor sat with John. He was deeply embarrassed, now claiming that he could only pay about half the reduced amount. The doctor asked if he had any family or friends who could come up with the remaining funds. John explained his situation. He was from the Mathare slum, without parents, and now without a job. He told the doctor that he promised to pay what he could and would not run out.

John's integrity was born not only out of newfound sense of decency but also out fear. The urban myth was that, if someone left the hospital without satisfying his account and was ever readmitted, he would be injected with poison. No matter how preposterous this might seem, it was effective. Hearing John's intentions, the doctor signed the discharge papers, allowing him to leave in three days and pay what he could.

The hospital stay was a time of reflection for John, from which was born a deep sense of gratitude, yet tinged by anxiety. As time drew near to his release, he'd wondered how he was going to start over once again. He had nothing. Worse yet, he was afraid, since his assailants were still at large. Once they knew he was on the streets again, would they try to finish him off before they fell prey to retributive justice dispensed by John and his friends?

Frightened though he was, John was deeply thankful. *God has made me pass through many challenges,* he thought to himself, *living in Good Samaritan, taking illegal alcohol, living on the street. Many of my friends slept on the streets like me, and I saw some die with glue bottles in their mouths. I have passed many hardships. I've been cut. But people encounter many storms. God helped me from the streets. I joined primary and secondary schools. I went to college. There are others like me who are living hopeless lives right now. But I'm alive. God knew all of this would happen to me, and yet he got me out of it. But please, dear Lord, I beg of you, don't make me live on the streets again, not on the streets again.*

Chapter 23
SHAVING MACHINE

As John left the hospital, he thanked the doctors and social workers for their care. He knew that he could have snuck out without paying a shilling. He simply would have asked his sister to bring his best clothes, changed into them, and walked out like a visitor. But wounded as he was, both physically and emotionally, he was determined to get a new start, so he paid what he could and departed.

John hurt deeply. He'd only had a few months left to finish his attachment and he could have moved on to study for a diploma. It never occurred to him to try to get back in touch with Kay. She certainly would have sympathized with the reason for the interruption of his internship. But to resume his studies, he would have had to get Kay's contact information through Mercy, and there was still bad blood between the two of them. Mama

Mercy had never wanted him to talk to Kay. John had received a scholarship only because he had drunkenly insinuated himself into their conversation and Kay was an open-minded, openhearted spirit looking to give young people a chance.

He was once again reduced to basics—Where was he going to live? He couldn't stay in Jane's room. It was already too crowded, and besides she and her family were struggling. There were times when her husband couldn't get work and the whole family went hungry. His aunts didn't want him. He couldn't rely on his old friends because they knew him as a drunkard and didn't want to deal with him. There was little choice but to go back to the video shop. He didn't want to be there, he wanted to be somewhere, somewhere with a future. He began to see Mathare for what it was—a place with no future. He thought to himself, *People live there and die there. You can say you're a millionaire, but deep down, you feel you are nobody living nowhere.*

*   *   *

Within the first weeks after returning to Mathare, his burden of fear lifted, as the fates of his assailants were determined. Two of the boys were caught in an attempted rape and sentenced to life in prison—in Kenya, an unimaginable hell. Two others caught trying to rob the Sunset Hotel in Eastleigh were gunned down on the spot. The boy shot in the knee went to a hospital and was eventually claimed by his uncle, who moved him to a rural area.

The sutures in John's head and arm were bothering him. As he healed, the twenty stitches across his crown began to pinch and itch. He had difficulty sleeping, especially on hard surfaces without a pillow to cradle his head. He could remove some stitches himself;

others would require professional assistance. He went to a local clinic, but without money, they wouldn't attend to him. As a last resort, he went to Kiumane. He explained the situation to Wangu, who took him to a Catholic mission clinic near the air base, handed over a few hundred shillings, and asked them to take care of him.

In addition to the cuts on his head, John had suffered a serious injury to his right hand and forearm. When he'd blocked the machete blow, the tendons in his arm had been partially cut. To restore some mobility, the surgeon had to fully cut the tendons and retie them. The operation left his three middle fingers with a restricted range of motion; only his thumb and little finger on his right hand regained full mobility. Recovery would be slow, perhaps a year and a half, and manual labor requiring heavy lifting— common work in the slums—was out of the question for the next six months. The doctors told him to keep the hand warm and the muscles loose—else amputation was a possibility.

So, John had to look for a simple job in Mathare. He thought about hawking at street corners, moving products of every description—bottled water, bananas, candies, kites, stuffed animals, three-legged stools, screwdrivers, and CD racks, whatever came available. But he really didn't want to do that.

Then he met Nahason Onyango, a strong, slender man, forty-five years old from the western Luo tribe, Kenya's second largest. Nahason earned his living pulling a handcart from the Eastleigh markets to Mathare, bringing vendors stocks of fruits and vegetables they would resell from their tiny street-side platforms. After an exhausting day's work, Nahason would plop himself at the Kiumane to unwind with a few glasses of changa'a. Sometimes he was so tired that he'd hand John money to run out and buy cigarettes, giving him one as a tip. Over time, they became friends. Nahason was impressed with John's work ethic, street smarts, and experience. They began to work together pulling handcarts, but that was difficult for John, who was still recuperating.

Then John introduced Nahason to the sewers. Nahason saw that it paid many times his work pulling carts and was far less strenuous. By now, the two were inseparable and John began to refer to his much older friend as "Baba Onyango," "Baba" being the familiar manner of addressing one's father.

At day's end, Nahason always enjoyed his drink and brought John along to the dens. John had not had a drink since he'd stopped during the first term at college in Limuru. Of course, there was no alcohol in the hospital, so he had gone over a year and a half without a drop. By October, however, only four months after his release from Kiambu, John was deep into drink.

Although John had sunk into alcohol yet again, Jane was there to support him. John gave her the keys to his newly rented room. Several times each week, she would go to John's place, wash his dirty clothes, and straighten up his quarters. If she found him asleep at night, she'd lock the door so no one would break in. Early the next morning, she'd come back to unlock it.

Occasionally, a friend would come by and tell Jane that her brother had passed out in a bar. She'd gather some of his buddies to carry him home. Sometimes she'd loan him money to pay rent, and if she saw a good bargain in the market, she'd buy him a piece of clothing.

But her generosity was not a one-way street. John would

frequently pass along some of his earnings from work in the sewers to help Jane and her husband take care of their family which had now grown to four children.

Because work was sporadic, when Nahason and John were at the bar, they would always buy drinks for their friends if they had money available. While it surely would have been prudent to put away the extra cash, rather than buying rounds for everyone, buying drinks for others was a unique way by which alcoholics saved money—buy for others today when you have funds, and they will buy for you when they're flush and you're low on cash.

One afternoon, Nahason and John were called urgently to fix a particularly difficult and dangerous problem. A dog had drowned in a twelve-foot deep manhole and blocked the flow of the drain. The effluent was backing up rapidly, and immediate attention was required.

Once on site, they quickly assessed the situation. Nahason stripped to his shorts and lowered himself into the cement cylinder. To reach the blockage, he had to hold his breath and lower himself beneath the rising water level. Out of breath, he surfaced; now it was John's turn to dive. Eventually, they successfully restored the flow of water, for which they received a huge payment of 4,500 shillings ($45).

Invigorated by their achievement and adrenalized by their exertion under perilous conditions, it was time to party. They went to Kiumane and bought gallons of changa'a, which was passed around to everyone in the room and anyone who walked in. After a night of revelry, John and Nahason somehow made it back to their respective quarters—John to the video shop and Nahason to his room in a nearby apartment building.

Late the next morning, John was rustled from his hungover slumber and told to get over to Nahason's room immediately.

Nahason's neighbors had heard him arrive late at night but had not detected any movement through the morning. When they finally entered his room, they found he had expired in bed. Not knowing how to locate his next of kin, they called John, who everyone knew was his closest friend.

When John entered the room, Onyango was in bed, his body cold. There was no light in his eyes; his face was frozen in a twisted scowl, his mouth contorted, giving the appearance that he'd died painfully.

John walked mournfully to the nearest police station in neighboring Pangani, where he had once been jailed. When he explained the situation, the police officers wanted a "tip" to take the body to the mortuary. Unable to meet their demands, John went over their heads to the OCS, who sympathized and ordered the patrolmen to remove the body.

Defiantly, John boarded the Land Cruiser with the two angry cops, which then crept along the packed Juja Road.

When they were within a few blocks of the apartment complex, the driver ordered John out of the vehicle, telling him to lead the way to the building. What ensued appeared to bemused onlookers as a low-speed chase, with John jogging ahead of a crawling police van.

When they finally arrived at Nahason's apartment building, several other drinking buddies were on the scene. Together with John, they carried Onyango's stiff corpse down the stairwell and loaded him onto the rear platform of the cruiser, the last they saw of their dear friend.

Why is death always so near to me? John thought. *How many times will death take my closest friends? Must I always walk in the shadow of death? Please, dear God, please show me Your good plans.*

* * *

Soon thereafter, another friend, Julius Sare, invited John to come to a barbershop he was renting. Cutting hair looked fun, not all that difficult, and certainly not too physically strenuous. Julius suggested that they pool their resources and open their own shop together.

John and Julius began assembling a small barber's kiosk. Neither of them had enough money to buy new materials or equipment, but they were able to cobble together used items and scraps to erect a simple shop next to Good Samaritan. John arranged the purchase of a secondhand electric clipper, or as he called it a "shaving machine." A cousin had clippers he wanted to sell but was asking 1,000 shillings ($10) which John thought was too rich. Knowing that his cousin would not negotiate with a relative, John found a friend to pretend to be interested in the apparatus. The fellow wangled the price down to 900 shillings ($9), which John reimbursed him plus 50 shillings for playing the part so well.

Julius found a large fragment of a mirror at a local dump and purchased a chair. John combed the streets and scrounged a section of gal sheet and some wood from recently burned structures. They scavenged the dregs of leftover paint buckets and mixed their own color for the exterior, a dull reddish brown. Over the course of a week, they constructed their tiny shop about five-foot-by-five-foot, just enough room for a seated customer and the barber. Anyone waiting had to stand outside in the street.

John in his barbershop

When he bought the clipper, John had no idea how to cut hair. He had never even held one on his hand, but he was determined to learn. Even if it only paid twenty or thirty shillings daily, John knew it would be worthwhile. He learned to cut hair by practicing on the orphan children from Good Samaritan. John was on a new track. His fervent prayer was, "God let me do something where no one will curse me."

Chapter 24
NEVER FORGOTTEN

About four months after his release from the hospital, John had resumed drinking. Although Julius had prevailed on him to reduce his consumption while cutting hair, John was still quite indulgent. He had been able to restore some dignity through steady work in the barbershop, but after three years of drinking, he was at a low point. His life seemed to have no meaning or direction. He felt the most vicious poverty, not the lack of material resources, but the lack of hope. He reflected, *I wanted to have a future.*

Inside, something was saying, *If you keep drinking, you will have no future.* He looked around and saw many younger than him who were living good lives. *And look at me. I am ashamed when I look back and remember how drunk I was when I went to Limuru. People had to hold my hand to lead me to the pickup point, and they had to carry the metal box of belongings when I arrived. I was even drunk when I did the entrance interview.*

He knew he had to stop. What ultimately drove John to stop drinking was not only the fear of missing out on a good future; it was also the fear that he may not have a future at all. John had seen too much death from alcohol. Just a few years ago, he had lost his very best friend, Nahason, and had carried his rigid corpse down a winding staircase. In the past year, two acquaintances had died in the video shop. Steven Murigi had gotten into a drunken brawl over some trivial matter and had been killed by a blow to the head with a pool cue. Willian Nzeki was a young lad who had been perpetually drunk for the past ten years. One night he went to sleep on a bench in the video shop next to John; he did not awaken the next morning. The autopsy determined that he had died of acute organ failure, at nineteen years of age.

Most gripping for John, however, was the memory of his mother. He could not bear to recall her pathetic demise—the stumbling, the shrieking, the banging, the violence, the uncontrolled weeping. His wonderful, loving Mum, whose life had ended like a stray animal in the gutters of 6th Street.

At that darkest moment, John chose life. Never since has he taken a drink.

In September 2013, he went to Kiumane and announced that he had stopped drinking. The patrons bellowed—how many times had Maina made that pronouncement? They mocked him—John, join us in a toast to your decision!

But this time, he kept to it. One week passed without a drink—and then two and then three. Word reached Mama Mercy, who went out of her way to congratulate him. Others joined, offering encouragement by purchasing him food.

John's life was turning around through the force of his own convictions. And his life would take another most unexpected turn when a taxi driver named Martin came to Good Samaritan.

* * *

Just a few days earlier in September 2013, Martin had picked up a white man, Paul Higdon, in the wee hours of the morning at Jomo Kenyatta International Airport. The connection had started out rather rough, but slowly a nascent friendship had formed. Eventually, the white man had volunteered that he wanted to find an orphan in Mathare he had not seen for twelve years.

Later that week, on his day off, Martin walked down to Good Samaritan as the man had requested. Passing through the gate, he met Mama Mercy and Nduku, the resident social worker and office assistant. Not recognizing Martin, they asked his business; was there a problem? Martin replied that he was looking for someone. Did they know a John Maina? They said they knew where to find him and that he should wait on a chair in the office. While they sent a young man to fetch him, Martin took a seat in the dank space, illuminated by a single bare hanging light bulb. Papers had overtaken the desk, and mounds of used clothes had overwhelmed every inch of available floor space.

In addition to operating his barbershop, John frequently cleaned the toilets at Good Samaritan and cared for the cows and assorted farm animals that were kept in pens across the street from the front gate. On the morning Martin showed up, he'd fed them a silage of napier grass and mucked out the stalls. He had just finished caring for the animals and returned to the video shop. He was watching a movie when the boy from Good Samaritan came in and told him that Nduku was looking for him. John wondered why she would beckon him. He had been there just a few minutes ago; the toilets were unblocked, and the animals were well fed. What could she want?

He followed the boy across the street to the office and saw a tall well-kempt man on a chair. Nduku asked if he knew Martin. John looked, trying to remember where he might have known him. He couldn't trace him to primary school or to secondary school, not to college, not to Mathare, Eastleigh, or Pangani. He confessed to Martin that they may have met, but he couldn't remember where.

Martin replied that they had never met and that he'd been sent by a white man from America called Paul Higdon who was looking for John Maina.

Perplexed, John turned the name over in his mind—*Paul Higdon … Paul Higdon*. He couldn't recall the name from the many guests who had visited Good Samaritan over the years.

Martin offered consolation, telling John that it had been almost twelve years since Higdon had been here, so of course it would be difficult to remember.

Now John was really puzzled. *Twelve years ago, and some American guy is looking for me now?* He told Martin to go back. Tell this man that John Maina is alive—that he still exists. He also requested that Higdon send a picture of himself.

* * *

That's when I received the text from Martin during a business meeting at Ripples in Meru— 'I found John Maina.' I couldn't believe what had happened. All these years and suddenly, only one month after proclaiming to Linda that I must find him, John had been found! Later that day, I picked up another text from Martin asking me to send a picture of myself. The only picture I had on file was the photo that Linda had taken of John and me just before boarding the van the day we met. How fitting that John and I should pick up again with an image of the last moments we had spent together twelve years ago.

* * *

The next day, Martin returned to Good Samaritan with the picture. When John saw it, he was shocked. *This is the man who I asked never to forget me!*

At that moment, he felt that God had come to his side. He thought to himself, *How could somebody remember me all those years? Why does he want to see me? How could this be happening?*

Chapter 25
MAY I COME WITH YOU?

In November 2013, Linda and I returned to Kenya. Along with us came her sister, Heidi, and her two sons, Isaac, a photography student at Columbia College in Chicago, and eight-year-old Lucas, who had been adopted by Heidi and her husband, Peter, two years ago from an orphanage in China. This was the family's first trip to Africa.

The reunion with John was planned weeks in advance of our trip through a series of emails between Martin and me. Since I didn't want to delay a moment longer than necessary, I arranged for us to go to Good Samaritan the morning after we made the transatlantic crossing.

To ensure all was in order, Martin went back to Mathare the afternoon before the meeting. John agreed to wait at his barbershop in front of the orphanage, but he still didn't believe Martin was telling the truth. He still wasn't entirely sure who the man in the picture was. After years on the street, his instincts wouldn't allow him to trust what was unfolding. He thought to himself, *Maybe Martin is cheating me. Is he really going to bring the guy in the picture?*

The next morning, the five of us jumped into the Toyota minivan that Martin had rented and made our way across the Central Business District. We crawled along Juja Road and then turned at the gas station where John and I had said farewell twelve years ago. It was no longer an abandoned Esso station, but a functioning Oil Libya petrol stop. The glistening white van, rarely seen in Mathare, turned down the road where John had first grabbed my hand as if he'd never let me go. The road was no longer the dirt track we had traversed but a well-paved, though still narrow street. We eked our way past the fruit wagons and makeshift stalls, which still lined the way as they had years ago. At the bottom of the long sloping hill we took a slow right turn, careful not to strike the children who were now gathering with curiosity around the vehicle.

My mind was a blank. Or maybe it was too full. I didn't know what to think. I was nervous with anticipation, wanting to see John but scared that this would be a silly fool's errand that would end in befuddled disappointment. I was scanning the crowd, landing on the face of every young man, trying to pick out John from the teeming street. Outwardly, I may have appeared calm; but inside, my heart was pounding, my mind racing.

* * *

John was standing in front of his barbershop and saw the van approaching. It stopped in front of Good Samaritan. John saw an older man through the windshield. *Could this really be the man in the photo?*

190

* * *

When I got out of the van, it was clear that John didn't immediately recognize me. I was a few pounds heavier and a few shades grayer.

He strode across the wide gutter; that's when he recognized me. Smiles broke across our faces. We hugged, three times.

But John seemed distant, standing a little too far away, not engaged, his eyes never fully meeting mine. I had expected a more voluble, joyous reception. I was thrilled; he seemed reserved. Our embraces seemed tentative. Whatever was in my mind was probably not in his. There was tension in the air and a sense of unease. After all, where do you pick up after twelve years?

We exchanged a few words—some hellos and how-are-yous. It seemed so trivial amid this improbable reunion. I decided to move things along by reintroducing John to Linda and then presenting Heidi, Lucas, and Isaac. I explained that this was their first trip to Africa and that we were taking them to see the various philanthropic sites upcountry in Meru at which we'd been working for the past twelve years. I recapped the itinerary, which included trips to game reserves and into the highlands. I told him we'd be gone for about a week, and we would see him again when we returned to Nairobi.

Still distant, standing patiently on the street taking it in, John responded with the line that opened my heart, "May I come with you?"

Hesitating only long enough to swallow, I immediately said, "Yes!"

I know spouses are supposed to check these things with each other. After all, inviting a relative stranger on a ten-day family holiday without consultation might cause one's spouse to raise an eyebrow. But Linda knew what this meant to me, and we both knew that, after coming all this way across all these years, we could not leave with a few hugs, superficial cordialities, and a quick tour through the orphanage. We agreed that John should join us. It was one of the most rewarding affirmations of life we have ever made. We had no idea of the worlds that were about to open to us.

John took us through Good Samaritan. The renovations from 2000 were still intact, but the play yard had been taken over by an imposing three-story cinder block structure. Donated by an NGO from Sacramento, California, the construction afforded more sleeping quarters for the burgeoning resident population, now over one hundred.

We were sure to stop in the office and greet Mama Mercy. Ever jovial, she was happy to see us, although clearly, she could not exactly place us after so many years and so many foreign visitors. Mercy, always the diplomat, complimented John, who she said was "a good boy." We toured the buildings, which John had taken me through in 2001, now in the shadow of the new edifice.

The boys' dormitory and the upstairs classrooms were exactly as they had been. What an eerie feeling to revisit the same rooms in virtually the same condition as that morning so long ago. Tingles of memory ran through my arms. My eyes moistened. I simply couldn't believe that I had found him—that I had returned to the site of an epiphany. I had absolutely no idea where this would lead. And that's the thrill of a new friendship.

After spending two hours together, we made plans to meet the next morning at a major traffic circle on the way up to Meru.

John and I reunited, November 2013
I am holding the picture Linda took of us in August 2001 as we were saying goodbye.

As our time closed and we boarded the van, John thought, *God is good. I just stopped drinking only a few weeks ago, and now there is this man who has come for me after all these years. He has come to remind me of the good things I was so close to but that never happened. Now I know, from this day forward, my life will not be the same again. God surely has good plans for me.*

We had arranged to meet at the bus stage near the Muthaiga Police Station. The station provided protective services for the community of Muthaiga, one of the most exclusive residential neighborhoods in Nairobi, which sits directly across the superhighway from Mathare.

John awoke early that morning, took tea at a local hotel, and packed his belongings in a small backpack. A few friends gathered around, congratulating him on his good fortune. Hoping to cash in on possible collateral benefits, two friends decided to accompany John to the stage.

We agreed to meet at 10:30 a.m. but were running late. While Kenyans are notoriously, habitually, chronically late by Western standards, it is well known that mzungus are always on time. We were running about an hour behind schedule. When we did not show up on time, doubts began to creep in. One of his friends began chiding John, saying it was all a hoax. "You're not going anywhere. No one's coming to get you. Let's just go back home," he grumbled.

Then I called John on his cell phone, apologizing and telling him to stay put; we were on our way. With all the traffic circling through the huge Muthaiga roundabout, John did not see the van until we were only a few yards away. I leapt out, gave him a hug, and saluted his friends, who were stunned by the entire affair.

We jumped in the van and were off to Meru.

Chapter 26
TOMORROW AND TOMORROW
AND TOMORROW

We zoomed along the newly refurbished Thika Road superhighway. This main thoroughfare leading north out of the city, along with all the major arterial roads running throughout Nairobi, had recently been reconstructed by the Chinese. As East Africa's leading political and economic country with a growing educated and prospering middle class, Kenya had attracted considerable attention and investment from many international quarters. Signs of the nation's increasing affluence were the many upscale malls that had been erected in the suburbs along these highways. Toward the northern edge of greater Nairobi, we stopped at the Thika Road Mall, TRM as it is known, to grab a quick dinner before heading into the remote upcountry.

Ascending the steep ramp to the rooftop parking lot, we made our way into the mall, whose shops lay beneath us down a long escalator. John had spent almost his entire life in the east end of Nairobi, in the contiguous neighborhoods of Mathare, Eastleigh, and Huruma. Occasionally, he'd venture to Pangani, adjacent immediately to the west. He had only been out of this small circle for the drama competition on the shores of Lake Victoria and to attend college in Limuru. He had never been in a mall, let alone a high-end shopping center like TRM. John carefully boarded the moving stairs and steadied himself for the ride down, exiting with a hiccup stumble. Once on the lower level, we noticed Funscapes, a small indoor bumper car arena, and decided to take a spin before dinner. It was an odd hour of the day; the mall was empty, and we were the only family riding the cars. What a glorious time we had spinning the steering wheels, wondering where those fanciful whirls would take us, aiming our cars at each other only to be pummeled from unexpected directions. It was the first time John was behind a wheel, and he got right into it, giving and getting just like the rest of us.

We filled up at Chicken Inn, whose slogan, "luv dat chicken," is just what Kenyans think about their favorite food, fried chicken. As we waited for our orders, I asked John how he liked the ride. "I wish we had taken pictures, so I could show the guys back in Mathare. I wasn't afraid of the cars, since I've seen children playing on them in movies. I figured anything that's safe for children isn't to be feared." Then he paused. "But that thing that moves people, that's scary. I've been in an elevator before but not one of those. It was fun riding, but at the bottom, I was afraid that my legs would get sucked under."

We had departed late from downtown Nairobi, and by the

time we left TRM, dusk was upon us. Our destination was Meru, the country's fifth largest city. Meru is located on the slopes of Mount Kenya, a seventeen thousand-foot extinct volcano and the second highest mountain in Africa. Its base is the largest in the world, some ninety miles in diameter. Mount Kenya is sacred in traditional Kenyan culture—the dwelling place of the gods, the creators and protectors of all that exists. Its craggy twin peaks are rarely scaled. It looms in the distance, and every time I circle its vastness, I too feel a sense of sacred presence beneath that remote bastion of fearsome beauty.

We had driven through darkness for four hours, and it was approaching 10:00 p.m. when we arrived in Nanyuki, a small regional city about an hour from Meru. We were tired and hungry, so we pulled into one of the reliable stops we knew along the route, a Nakumatt shopping center, a national retail chain in Kenya along the lines of Target stores. Nakumatts were rather upscale by African standards, situated in clean, well-kept, unremarkable shopping centers, not unlike the clean, well-kept, unremarkable shopping centers in the United States. This Nakumatt was located just off the busy two-lane highway that circles Mount Kenya.

We pulled into the parking lot, a modest space accommodating some twenty to thirty vehicles. We intended to make a brief rest stop at clean facilities and grab a snack at an all-night coffee shop. Not many creatures were stirring on the streets of Nanyuki. The security guard raised the barrier as soon as he saw foreigners—no questions asked. Aspiring to present itself as an upscale establishment, Nakumatt's parking lot was surrounded by a tall iron fence, separating its esteemed clientele from the coarser townies.

As we climbed down from the van, we saw two gaunt, wraith figures clutching the fence. Filthy sweatshirts and baggy jeans hung on their wiry frames. Wan faces stared at us. Lucas spotted them first, two kids not much older than him. Lucas had been in the van with adults all day, so here was a chance for some much-needed camaraderie. He ran to the fence. The boys were puzzled to see a small Chinese kid confidently striding up to them. John followed right behind. The four talked while the adults used the facilities and grabbed a quick bite to eat. The two boys at the fence were bemused by the garrulous Chinese kid barraging them with questions about their lives. Finally, they turned to John and inquired in their native language if this child could possibly help them. John said the boy couldn't, but his mother, aunt, and uncle could.

It was good fortune to have John along, since the boys spoke only a little English. In his native Kikuyu tongue, John determined that their names were Robert and George and that they were street boys. They told John that they thought they were about ten or eleven years old and had been living on the streets of Nanyuki for about three or four years. They said that they often hung out at Nakumatt, hoping the rich shoppers would give them some food or money.

The adults joined the four boys. John and Lucas told us what they had learned about their new acquaintances. It was late, and we had only wanted to stop for a few minutes. But Heidi, Linda, and I decided we couldn't just drive away and leave these two boys, so we motioned them to take the walkway opening through the fence. The guard gave a start; we assured him that all was well. We invited the boys to sit with us in the café. Linda and Heidi took charge and helped them pick out hot meat pies and soft drinks, which they devoured in the shop's shabby but comfortable leather chairs.

Speaking through John, in their native tongue they slowly, shyly told us more about their lives on the streets. Their days were spent wandering through Nanyuki looking for food. Places like Nakumatt were great because they'd come to know some of the patrons, who would regularly toss them a few shillings. Since yesterday morning, though, they hadn't eaten more than a few scraps. They were just finishing up the night, taking one final turn past Nakumatt and hoping to scrounge some last morsels before going to sleep.

"Where do you sleep?" Linda asked them.

"There's a bank just down the street, and there's some soft grass behind the bushes, so we're kind of hidden. What's great is that's there's a night guard who sits out front. He watches the bank. Sometimes we give him money to make sure he protects us from the older boys."

At this point, Heidi and I were overcome by emotion; we both walked away. Heidi wept mother's tears of horror—Robert and George were only a few years older than Lucas, living alone on the streets. My heart began opening to these boys. I clenched my jaw tightly, fighting back the tears and struggling to maintain some sense of composure. I had occasionally read about children living in these conditions, but I had no real sense of the life of a street boy. Now two were right beside me. I was looking brokenness in the face. These were not kids in a newspaper article or film documentary. We were not floating past them in an air-conditioned vehicle. Here sat two young boys scratching their ways through life, day after precarious day—horizons no further than the next bit of food; dreams of a better life, of home, of school, choked by the need to survive. Today was all that mattered; tomorrow was too far off to be concerned.

Heidi and I grabbed Linda and decided more had to be done. How could we possibly feed these boys, have a nice conversation, and then send them on their way? The ladies saw that they needed new clothes. We decided to scrap our plans for the next day and asked John to translate for us--we're coming back tomorrow afternoon to buy you new clothes. By now, the boys had shed their initial wariness. Words flowed more freely. They were starting to warm up to us. They agreed to meet us tomorrow at the Nakumatt parking lot at one o'clock.

To end the night, we offered them a ride to the bank about half a kilometer down the highway. We gave each of them 200 shillings so they could buy breakfast and lunch the next day. As we pulled up to the branch, we saw the night watchman slumped asleep in his plastic chair, silhouetted against the buzzing glow of incandescent blue and green commercial signage.

John and Lucas got out of the van with George and Robert. Without prompting from the adults, the four spontaneously locked arms, bent over in a huddle, and began to pray. I could just make out the words; they were giving thanks for the bounty of newfound friendships and hope for meeting tomorrow. Again, I clenched my jaw as hard as I could, holding back the emotions of the touching scene—four boys, all with hardscrabble lives, pausing to recite the Lord's Prayer and giving thanks for the simple gifts of the evening. Robert and George walked slowly across the lawn. Then they slid behind the bushes into their shrub sanctuary.

We continued our journey through the enveloping darkness. I turned to John. I knew very little about his life, just something about his time in the orphanage and a bit about his years on the street. I asked what it meant to him to meet Robert and George.

When he saw the boys, John said he'd flashed back to the streets, remembering his former life. He told me how he used to beg at the roundabout for a few shillings just to get a piece of bread before starting school. Sullenly, John reflected that so many people would just look at him dismissively and say, "Tomorrow," pretending to make a pact with him to return the next day. That word hurt because he knew they would never come back. When Robert and George greeted him, he felt helpless because he didn't have anything to give to them. So, when he saw me coming, he was worried that, because he'd only seen me use credit cards, I wouldn't have any cash to give them, and they would feel rejected just as he had at the roundabout.

There was a long pause. Then John told me that, as the boys walked to the bushes, he felt hopeful: "If you had been thinking of me all those years, I knew in my heart these children will be better off than me. They only have to wait one more day, just till tomorrow."

* * *

It had been an emotionally draining end to a long day. So many feelings washed through me. Over the years, I've reflected on that events of the evening. What did I think I would accomplish by coming back the next day to clothe these two young men? Did I think I was going save them? Would Robert and George really be all that much better off with a few new clothes? And what about all those years of work at Ripples—was that done just to assuage a barrenness in my own soul? What did I think my occasional contributions were going to amount to? Was all this work in Kenya really going to add up to anything more than a bunch of good stories to tell back home?

Then a clear, bright sense arose within me. I could dwell on these doubts to my dying day, paralyzed in search of just the right gesture born only of the purest motives. Or I could firmly grasp the one thing I was sure of—there were children out there who needed help, and I was able to make a difference in their lives.

As I came to learn, the path of service is not without its challenges. When we encounter privation, it is all too easy to look away—to recoil from life's ugliness. There have been embarrassingly too many occasions on which I have walked away. Emotionally closing down feels safe, and I have chosen emotional safety more than I care to admit. I have turned my gaze from human suffering, seeking refuge in spiritual complacency. Fearful of feeling hurt, I have sought the security of mute comfort.

But I slowly came to discover that great rewards come from opening one's heart to all of life—its transcendent joys and ubiquitous suffering, embracing the happenstance of privileged circumstance, along with the casualty of unfortunate birthplace. None of us will ever alleviate the world's suffering, but we can contribute to making it better.

PART V
AFTERWORD
—— 2014–2018 ——

I know we're all pretty small in the grand scheme of things.
And I suppose the most you can hope for
is to make some kind of difference.
But what kind of difference have I made?
What in the world is better because of me?

—Warren Schmidt (played by Jack Nicholson)
in the movie, *About Schmidt*

Chapter 27
A LITTLE BOOST

In November 2014, one year after our reunion with John, Linda and I helped him move out of the Mathare slum to the more pleasant climes of Meru, on the slopes of Mount Kenya. He now lives in a clean, spacious single-room wooden hut, adjacent to which sits his business, the "Illinois Barber Shop."

Linda and I continue to visit Kenya, usually twice a year. On each occasion, we are sure to spend lots of time with John. Intrigued by fragments of John's story she had heard over the years, one afternoon in 2015, Linda asked him to sit with her in the lobby of our hotel in Meru and tell her about himself. Always an avid note taker, she came away with a dozen typewritten pages. On returning home, she shared them with me. I was immediately captivated by John's roller-coaster life.

Starting in 2016, I began working with John to write his life's story, which has become this book. Rather than just interview him, we spent countless hours walking through Eastleigh and Mathare, visiting those places that were important in his life. During our walks, John told me many tales, and there are three that beautifully capture his spirit. One of the first locations he took me was a special place in his life, so unlike the teeming slum in which he spent most of his youth.

* * *

Beneath the hill on which the Mathare Mental Hospital sits, lies a ten-acre wetland buffering the bustling residential and commercial district of Mathare from the Thika Road superhighway. The wetland is formed by several small creeks, which come together a few hundred yards downstream to form the Mathare River. Although the creeks are not nearly as foul as the river, no outdoor running water in the greater Nairobi region is unpolluted.

John explained that he used to bathe in these waters. It was a typical warm, sunny day when we arrived at the spot. We watched one young man clean himself as John had done years ago. The tall strapping lad was sitting in a running creek only a bit wider than his body. He was surrounded by slender green wetland grasses, beautifully contrasted against his black arms, torso, and shaved head. Rich white foam billowed as he lathered himself with soap. He scrubbed with a cloth held diagonally across his back from shoulder to waist, which John explained was an old piece of flour sack. Cupping his hands, he'd fill them with water, which he'd quickly hoist to rinse himself.

While some were bathing, others were washing their clothes, lying them atop the grasses to dry in the sun. Boys and girls alike bathed here, although always in separate areas. John said that he'd come down here twice each month to clean himself and wash his clothes. In the interim, he'd try to clean up at the showers of the public toilet block, but all too often it had no water.

Viewing the site with the eyes of an American obsessed with personal hygiene, I was appalled at people washing in these streams. I blurted, "How can you possibly wash in this dirty water?"

Not at all bothered by bathing in the river, he thought I was concerned for his clothes. Talking by each other, he offered me a response that I did not expect, "It didn't bother us. See, street boys only wear dark clothes, not white ones. So, there's no problem at all."

Beyond the mere practicality of cleanliness, however, this spot had a profound meaning for John. Far from the congestion and tension of life in Mathare, amid fields of green and nothing but the sky above, John experienced a sense like nowhere else. He reflected wistfully, "I started coming here when I was six years old. I'd come twice a week. I would just sit in the water the whole day if I wanted. This was the only place where I had the freedom to do what I wanted. It was the only place I really felt free."

* * *

On another occasion, we were walking along the street in front of Good Samaritan, which prompted me to ask him what he remembered from the day we met in August 2001.

John clearly remembered that day. Early that morning, Mama Mercy had called together about a dozen older boys, telling them that visitors were coming. She explained that it was a group from Chicago, and the boys would have to go up the hill to the old Esso station to escort them back to Good Samaritan.

He remarked that, as they made their way up the hill, he saw me standing by the van. His first impression from afar was, "You looked like someone who was waiting for the next step, so I took your hand." He paused and added, "Somehow I knew that I would have to take you back up the hill."

He recalled pointing out the boys in the river and the cries of the little children—wazungu, wazungu! —as we reached the entrance of Good Samaritan.

He told me he felt angry when we reached the gate because he thought he would never talk to me again. He explained that Mama Mercy did not want anyone talking with visitors because she wasn't sure what they would say about the home. Most visitors spent their time with Mercy and never came back. But that day, he decided to break the rules and take me around Good Samaritan. He felt uncomfortable because he didn't speak English very well but really wanted me to be impressed with his home.

When his tour was over, he was concerned because he wasn't supposed to take visitors back up the hill; usually a different group of boys would do that. But he decided he was going to walk back with me to the petrol station, even if he had to hide and catch up with me later. When Mama Mercy said he could walk back with me, it made him happy.

He became somber as he described those last few minutes together. "When we got to the top of the hill, I remember you asking me what I wanted to be when I finished school. No visitor had ever asked me that. I told you I wanted to be a lawyer.

"Just then I felt hope. I wanted to create hope somewhere, so I asked you never to forget me. I had never said that to anyone else.

"Then Mum" (Linda) "took a picture of us together, and I heard you say my name. You got in the van, and the doors locked. That's when I became sad again. I waved goodbye and saw you looking at me until the traffic got in the way.

"My last thought was, *God knows*. That's what I knew in my heart."

* * *

I felt there was something else John had to tell me; he was holding something in. A while later, it all came out.

In October 2017, John told me that he found an unexpected message posted on his Facebook page. A lady named Shiro asked if he was related to her brother, Irungu. One of her Facebook searches had led her to John Maina Thuo, which sounded like it could be one of her nephews. Startled, John replied that it was possible. To make sure, Shiro arranged a phone call with him. After fielding a probing battery of questions, Shiro confirmed that John was indeed the son of her brother, James Irungu. She explained that a family reunion was planned for early December, and she was trying to round up as many relatives as she could find.

Now that they had found each other, John asked if he could spend some time with her before the big gathering. She invited him to visit her in Nanyuki, the city where we met Robert and George, the street boys.

John did not recall Shiro from his youth, and it was nice to finally meet a welcoming relative. Shiro fondly recalled how she used to hold baby John. She explained that Irungu was the oldest of seven siblings. The younger ones came to love him since he looked out for them, often walking them to school in the morning.

John solemnly offered vague, sporadic memories of his father. He told her of the demise of Keziah and being forced onto the streets. Finally, he asked balefully, "Why didn't you come looking for us?"

Shiro offered no reply and continued with her story.

After Irungu left Keziah and the family, she recounted, he remarried and had three children, the oldest a boy also named John. The family lived in Kayoli, a lower-class community just east of Mathare, one notch above a slum. One afternoon, Irungu came home to find John lying motionless in a ditch of stagnant water. He could see that an overhead electrical line had fallen into the puddle. The thirteen-year old boy had been electrocuted. Irungu was despondent; he had lost another John.

* * *

On the evening of December 2, 2017, the family convened at Irungu's mother's house in Murang'a. John and a distant cousin rode in the same matatu from Nairobi, which dropped them at a country lane about one mile from the matron's homestead. As they walked along the dirt road, they passed an older man with white hair and a white beard. The gentleman greeted them politely. They paused for an instant and then kept walking. The man continued, "Do I know you from somewhere?"

John and his cousin looked at each other, back at the man, and then at each other again and responded, "No."

The young men resumed their stride. Then came the unexpected question, "Maina, do you know who I am?"

John glanced over his shoulder, more to look for his cousin, who was trailing behind rather than to acknowledge the stranger.

"I am your father."

John didn't flinch or break stride; he and his cousin continued apace, impervious to the man's gratuitous declaration.

When they arrived at their grandmother's home, Jane was waiting. She was exhausted from shepherding her four children along the hilly country road.

The house was situated in a large compound with several dwellings built by family members. Irungu had a spacious three-bedroom home inside the walls.

The reunion began with all introducing themselves and explaining their relation to others in the family. When it came to Irungu, he stated quietly, with a recognizable tinge of shame, that he was the father of John and Jane. Impassive, neither of them looked his way.

Soon it was Jane's turn. She boasted to be the proud mother of two boys and two girls and the loving sister of John. John was next, and he announced himself as the proud uncle of the four and the loving brother of Jane. Neither uttered a word about Irungu.

After the introductions were finished, John strode up to Irungu and challenged him to prove he was their father. Irungu did not offer any explanation other than to say he would make everything clear the next time they meet. With that, Irungu excused himself from the party, claiming he had to return urgently to Nairobi.

* * *

John related this story to me with equanimity, devoid of rancor. I asked him how he felt meeting his father for the first time in more than thirty years.

"Nothing, I felt nothing, Dad," he said to me. "There was no satisfaction in hearing him say I'm his son. The one who takes care of me, that's my dad."

John and I today

* * *

Since John and I were improbably, perhaps miraculously reunited in 2013, we have been together ever since. We are now more than friends. African custom prizes personal bonds above the precision of bloodlines, so in a true African sense we have become father and son. Linda and I have been the only adults who have consistently been there to support him. What an honor to be John's Mum and Dad. How blessed we are to call John our son, along with our own two boys, Lars and Nils.

As we worked together on this book, John openly shared with me his memories. While this book is the story of John's life and survival on the streets of Mathare, it is also the story of the spiritual inspiration we have both experienced through the friendship we have developed. John showed me a world of human dignity where I never would have thought to look. From him, I have learned profound lessons of resilience, perseverance, courage, and faith—uplifting lessons of character forged in a world few of us encounter, with challenges more overwhelming than most of us can imagine, qualities of character in sharp contrast to his material circumstances.

Mark Twain has mused, "The two most important days of your life are the day you were born and the day you know why." One brilliant sunny morning in the slums of Nairobi, I met John Maina and experienced the first inklings of the difference that I could make. For me, it was my second most important day, the day on which I first began to know why.

* * *

After all he's been through and after all the stories he's told me, I asked John if he thought he's had a happy life.

"I don't *think*, I *know* I've had a happy life!" he exclaimed without hesitation. "I was shaving the other day in Mathare, and someone came up to me and asked, 'Maina, is that you? I thought you were dead.' People never believed I'd ever leave Mathare—certainly not alive. Yes, Dad, I'm supposed to be a past tense by now.

"I've also had a successful life. I have my own business. I don't have to beg. I live my own life. I'm my own boss. I don't have to have a building or car or a plot of land to be successful.

"There are many people in Mathare who had better dreams than me. They wished to be doctors or pilots, and they tried their level best. But no one gave them a boost. That's what most of us need, Dad, just a little boost."

APPENDIX A:
WHAT HAPPENED TO THE OTHERS?

Mama Mercy is very special to Linda and me. We visit her at Good
Samaritan every time we go to Nairobi. She recently turned
sixty years old and is still busy taking care of orphaned children.
At last count there were 295 souls under her care—125 in
primary school, 110 in secondary, and 60 at technical colleges
and universities. She always takes us to her room, where there's a
mattress on the floor. That's where she sleeps, cradling newborns
recently rescued from the street.

I knew John had had a difficult relationship with Mercy,
almost from the start, so I asked how things were going between
them. Since John stopped drinking and moved to Meru, he

and Mercy have reconciled. Mercy respects him for overcoming alcoholism and putting his life in order. Whenever he returns to Nairobi, she invites him to dinner. He cleans the toilet block for free as his donation to the center.

Jane, John's sister. Recently, Jane's husband left her for another woman. She and her four children had to leave their comfortable suite and now occupy a single cramped room with plastic tarp walls and a leaking roof. Jane supports her family by hawking bottled water at traffic lights in downtown Nairobi. John talks with Jane frequently and visits her every time he's in Nairobi.

Daniel, John's half brother, is a manager at Digital Data Divide, one of the many technology firms that has grown up in Nairobi's "Silicon Savannah." John has not seen Daniel in over ten years. Recently, John contacted Daniel and told him about our book. The three of us are going to have dinner together the next time I'm in Kenya.

Victor Maregwa, his roommate and drinking partner at the Desert Dew. Victor's dream to get off the streets did not come true. He earns his daily living by hauling water up the stairws of tall apartment buildings in Eastleigh. Victor can no longer afford a room of his own; he sleeps against a municipal sewerage line, which provides him warmth on cold Nairobi nights.

Margaret Muthoni, John's girlfriend through primary and secondary school, works for Revlon Professional as a cosmetician.

Simon Mwangi, Mama Mercy's son. From 2003 through 2010, Simon worked in Dubai as a security guard for a hotel. He recently returned to Mathare, married, and lives in one of the upper floors of the new addition to Good Samaritan.

Martin, the taxi driver who found John, married an American and now lives in the US working as a delivery driver.

Mrs. Maina, John's secondary school teacher, was transferred to the prestigious State House Girls Secondary School, one of the finest in the country.

Robert and George, the street boys we met in Nanyuki. Within one week after meeting at the Nakumatt, we were able to place them in a home for orphans and vulnerable children in Meru. After a few months, George ran away and returned to the streets. After four and a half years of excellent performance in school, Robert fell into drug use, left the home, dropped out of school and made his way back to Nanyuki, where he is living on the streets again.

Peter Musyoki, head boy at Good Samaritan married a nurse. Together, they opened a chemist shop (pharmacy).

Kapufi ("Shorty"), who lived with John in the Kiumane changa'a den, died several months ago from years of excessive alcohol consumption. His body was found by the police in a dumpster. His remains lay in the city mortuary for nearly one month, until distant relatives came from the countryside to bring him back to his ancestral home to be buried.

Mudu Muriu ("Blackie"), who also lived with John in the Kiumane, still works in the changa'a den, where he has slept every night for the last nineteen years.

Steven Kamigi, who rescued John from the assailants, gave up theft in 2016 when he got married. He did, however, use his ill-gotten proceeds to set his wife up with a fully stocked kiosk in Mathare. Now on the straight and narrow, Steven is a garbage man serving the Eastleigh community.

Gitari's Band

Mouo sells mangos at the 12th Street Bus stage in Eastleigh.

Steven Kivindu died with a glue bottle in his mouth.

Vincent Ochieng is a member of a troop that performs traditional African dances. He also assists his sister in her beauty salon.

Gitari. John tried to locate him in the Mukuru kwa Ruben slum where he had been living. Neighbors told John that Gitari had been hit by a car and confined to a wheelchair. Word has it that he was moved back to Murang'a, where an aunt is taking care of him. John and I are determined to find him. Gitari is someone I have to meet.

APPENDIX B:
TIMELINE OF JOHN'S LIFE

1983	Born December 12 in Nairobi
1984-88	Lives with his mother, half brother, and sister in a flat in Eastleigh
1988	Attends kindergarten at St. Theresa's Catholic school
	His mother, Keziah, is committed to the Mathare Mental Hospital
	Year end—Keziah abandons the family; John and Daniel take to the streets
1989-91	John and Daniel live on the streets of Eastleigh with Gitari's band
1991	August—John and Daniel taken in by Mama Mercy

1991-2002	John lives in Mama Mercy's orphanage, Good Samaritan
1993-98	Attends Huruma Primary School
1999	Enters Maina Wanjigi Secondary School
2001	John and Paul meet at Good Samaritan orphanage
2002	John completes secondary school; immediately dismissed from Good Samaritan
2003-08	Lives in Kiumane changa'a den and CHE Mathare video shop
2009	Studies at Limuru Agricultural Youth Centre
2010	January—begins attachment at Kuguru Food Complex February—attacked by a gang June—released from Kiambu District Hospital August—with Julius, opens barbershop adjacent to Good Samaritan
2011-12	Lives in CHE Mathare video shop while operating barbershop
2013	September—Martin, the taxi driver, finds John November—John and Paul are re-united; John travels with Paul's family
2014	November—moves to Meru
2017	Family reunion; John meets his father for the first time in 30 years

APPENDIX C:
SWAHILI & ENGLISH GLOSSARY

English

attachment	internship
hotel	an eatery serving tea or a full-scale menu
OCS	officer commanding station; head officer at the local police station
prefect	student classroom monitor; also, the steward in a beer den
preps	after-class study sessions in preparation for national exams
spark	a magnet
stage	bus stop for multiple routes
tea	hot morning drink plus bread

Swahili

bhang	marijuana
changa'a	illegal alcohol, moonshine
chapati	fried bread, a Kenyan tortilla
chokara	literally filthy person; derogative name for street boys
githeri	traditional Kenyan dish of beans and maize
jembe	hoe
mandazi	Swahili doughnut
manyweti	drunkard
matatu	bus
mzee	esteemed elder gentleman
mzungu	white foreigner
nyama choma	roasted meat
panga	machete
panya route	literally "rat track"
taka-taka	garbage
ugali	African polenta
wanachi	common Kenyan citizens
wazungu	plural of *mzungu*

ACKNOWLEDGMENTS

There are so many to whom I owe thanks in many different measures. I would like to thank my instructors and classmates at the Writer's Studio of the University of Chicago for their candid comments and encouragement during the earliest stages of composition. Thanks also to George Kamau and Shelly Kacergis for reading the full manuscript and providing recommendations that made a difference. An extra thanks to George for some great photography and videography of the Mathare slum. My technical partners are superb: Sabrina Sutton of A+ Graphics and Kellie Bambach of Sparklefurry. Ed Castro of Gadget Web Design created my websites and runs my social media campaign.

Within my own family, there is no way to repay my departed parents, Nana and Padley, who gave me opportunities they never had. As an author I deal in words, yet words cannot express what our two sons, Lars and Nils, and our daughter-in-law, Brei, mean in my life.

There are five individuals who made this book possible.

First is Professor Kay whose NGO provided essential support for many years to orphans living in Good Samaritan and sponsored John to attend technical college. Thank you for giving so many young people a chance in life.

Martin, the taxi driver. Thank you, Martin, for staying with that surly old man early one morning at the Nairobi airport. Thank you for opening yourself to the strange request to find an orphan I had not seen in twelve years. Without your generosity of spirit, I don't know if I ever would have found John.

Kevin Davis, my teacher and editor. Thank you, my friend, for your professionalism and patience. How far we've come together from that scrawny little booklet I first served up to you!

John, I hope what I've written is the testimonial you deserve, my son. You have opened my eyes to a world I never would have found and you've inspired in me a sense of the boundless dignity of humanity.

Finally, it is to Linda, to whom this book is dedicated, that I owe the greatest thanks. Not only did we discover Africa together, we found each other and continue each day to discover what lies within each of us. To you, Linda, I owe whatever sensitivity and insight this volume offers, because you have helped draw it out of me.

We wrap ourselves in a quilt of relationships, some transient and fortuitous, others lifelong and profound. Through these bonds with others our lives are graced with hope and a future.

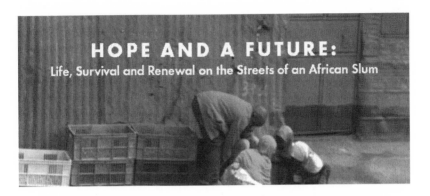

HOPE AND A FUTURE:
Life, Survival and Renewal on the Streets of an African Slum

I invite you to sign up for my newsletter
at **www.paulhigdon.net**
You'll receive colorful photos, first hand stories,
and details about Little Boost projects for kids.

LITTLE
BOOST
PRESS

Made in the USA
Monee, IL
05 May 2020